Rachel Dwyer is Professor of Indian Cultures and Cinema at SOAS, University of London. She teaches undergraduate and postgraduate courses and supervises PhD research on Indian cinema. Her books include *All You Want is Money, All You Need is Love: Sex and Romance in Modern India*; *Pleasure and the Nation: the History and Politics of Public Culture in India* (co-edited with Christopher Pinney); *The Poetics of Devotion: The Gujarati Lyrics of Dayaram*; *Cinema India: The Visual Culture of the Hindi Film* (co-authored with Divia Patel); *Yash Chopra*; *100 Bollywood Films*; and *Filming the Gods: Religion and Hindi Cinema.*

SERIES EDITOR: TONY MORRIS

What Do
HINDUS
Believe?

Rachel Dwyer

Granta Books
London

Granta Publications, 12 Addison Avenue, London W11 4QR
First published in Great Britain by Granta Books 2008

A CIP catalogue record for this book is available
from the British Library.

1 3 5 7 9 10 8 6 4 2

ISBN 978 1-86207 861 1

Typeset by M Rules
Printed and bound in Great Britain by
J. H. Haynes & Co. Ltd., Sparkford

For my teachers
gurubhyo namaḥ

Contents

Acknowledgements

I am particularly grateful to Christopher Shackle and Michael Dwyer for their detailed comments, critical readings and editorial work on drafts of this book. My editor at Granta, Bella Shand, has shaped this book with exceptional acuity and enthusiasm.

My great thanks are due as ever to Jerry Pinto, who conducted interviews with Chirodeep Chaudhuri and Santosh Thorat in July 2006. Thanks also to Chirodeep Chaudhuri, Faisal Devji, Amitaben Lalitchandra Patel, Maithili Rao, Santosh Thorat and Kush Varia.

1

Hindu and Hinduism

Hinduism is the third-largest religion in the world with around one billion followers – though some place it higher at 1.4 billion,* making it almost the same size as Islam and smaller only than Christianity.

Most Hindus (around 900 million) live in India and in its neighbouring countries: Nepal is the only officially Hindu state in the world (where 80 per cent of the 23 million population is Hindu), and Hindu minorities are found in Pakistan (3 m), Sri Lanka (3 m) and Bangladesh (15 m). Other substantial communities are found in areas of old migration from India, such as Indonesia (4.5 m) and Malaysia (1.5 m), while later migrations have seen Hindus settle in Africa, Europe, North and South America.

Hinduism is one of the world's oldest and largest religions, yet it is also one of the hardest to define as it shares few of the features of other major religions. There is no founder, no single scripture nor any central organization. It has no core belief,

*Clarke, Peter B. (ed.) (1993) *The Religions of the World: Understanding the Living Faiths.* Marshall Editions Limited: USA: 125.

and allows for atheism, polytheism and monotheism. Hindu practices vary widely across social groups and regions, and Hindus do not always share the same key festivals and rituals. The Europeans, who first came to India several centuries ago, doubted that Hinduism was even a religion because it was so different from their own Judeo-Christian religions, not being a 'faith' with a belief in god at its core.

However, there are certain core beliefs that Hindus share, such as transmigration or reincarnation where the soul is reborn after death. Most Hindus avoid eating beef and revere the Vedas and the Bhagavad Gita, key Hindu texts. Hindus are born into the complex system of caste, whereby groups of people are divided into separate delineations, who can only remain ritually pure according to their relations with other caste groups. Caste affects one's choice of occupation and marriage partner. These features are shared by other religions in India: Jains believe in reincarnation, Sikhs do not eat beef and Muslims and Christians observe the demands of caste. Defining Hinduism, then, is a complex task, based on a variety of beliefs, practice and social behaviour. No core belief is definitive, and a Hindu may reject caste or be of mixed caste, may eat beef, or not know any of the sacred texts or participate in rituals.

The terms 'Hindu' and 'Hinduism' are found relatively late in the long history of religious beliefs and practices in India. The word 'Hindu' was first used by Persian speakers to refer to anyone who lived in India, the land to the east of the Sindhu (the River Indus), and which meant simply 'Indian'. The word 'Hinduism' has been translated into many other Indian languages as *Hindu dharma* or *sanatana dharma*, which means something like 'eternal religion'. Until the nineteenth century, there was no single term used to describe the religious groups that might now be called Hindu, and indeed many words which describe what we might call 'sects' are still used in preference to or alongside the word Hindu. This absence of a single term used by all Hindus to describe their religious beliefs and practices reflects widespread uncertainty: is there a single religion called Hinduism, or is it a term best used to describe a group of religions?

Whatever the scholarly debates, the term 'Hindu' has come into common use over the last two centuries, though its meaning may differ according to circumstances. For example, the term first coined for political purposes in the nineteenth century has been employed in the Indian constitution to define the religious community. In social use, Hindus may use the term to non-Hindus to define themselves as members of a larger group, whereas among themselves they would also give their sectarian name, caste name or regional name. So a Hindu from the Punjab, who is Khatri by caste and a follower of the Arya Samaj might say she is 'Hindu' or 'Arya Samaji', 'Hindu Khatri' or 'Hindu Punjabi' according to the context.

Jainism, Sikhism and Buddhism are often grouped as varieties of Hinduism in India, although they are generally regarded as distinct religions by their followers. Hinduism shows such awareness of other religions and sects to the extent that one of its key beliefs is this acknowledgement of diversity and difference while recognizing that all religions are ultimately one.

The coining of the words 'Hindu' and 'Hinduism' show how much the concept of Hinduism was defined from outside before it was internalized by Hindus themselves.

In India one is identified by the government as Hindu by birth, whether one wants it or not, as there is no uniform civil legal code. Caste, ascribed at birth and acknowledged by caste associations and by other caste members, is recognized by the government who allocate university places, jobs and other government positions to low castes. One cannot 'stop being a Hindu' as there is no repudiation of faith one can make other than conversion, a course of action which has been followed by many of the Dalits (once known as Untouchables) who have become neo-Buddhists.

One is born a Hindu, so Hinduism does not grow through conversion. It is not technically possible to convert to Hinduism, but outsiders may join certain groups, which follow key Hindu beliefs. Not all Hindus accept these converts as Hindus. The Hare Krishnas, followers of ISKCON, the International Society for Krishna Consciousness, who are mostly Western converts, are not recognized as Hindus for certain ritual functions such as marriage as they have no caste status, despite their orthodox practices and beliefs.

Hinduism's fluid social and cultural forms have proved popular with the younger generation of Indians who take an active role in temple worship and Hindu youth organizations as well as participating in internet communities. They may select their own blend of beliefs and practices such as observing fasts and vegetarianism, or taking up astrology and yoga, while rejecting more traditional beliefs in caste, such as the supremacy of Brahmins and doctrines of Untouchability. Others join new sects founded by gurus and godmen who offer forms of Hinduism more appropriate to their modern lives.

Despite the antiquity of Hinduism, its wonderful myths and stories appeal to modern children. For forty years, English-reading Indians have enjoyed the *Amar Chitra Katha*, comic-strip stories based on the ancient texts, and the original stories can now be found on the internet and in films and television programmes. In addition to religious belief, many are involved with identity politics, defining themselves as Hindu in the face of a global Islamic resurgence, while others enjoy cultural activities from an aesthetic point of view: music, costume, dance, cuisine and decoration, while the temples and caste associations offer opportunities for language courses, social meetings and activist organizations.

Hinduism's seemingly endless flexibility and diversity is proving to be one of its major strengths, as India undergoes the most rapid social and economic changes in its history.

Hindu belief allows Hindus to live in the modern and the pre-modern worlds simultaneously. For example, Hindu practitioners of Western medicine who understand the science of physiology may well prefer to treat themselves and their families with traditional Indian Ayurvedic remedies which are not 'scientific' or 'modern'.

Hinduism's familiar rituals and ceremonies provide stability in a time of change, while its beliefs offer new answers to new problems. Hindus believe that the world is sacred, and new discourses about global warming and ecological issues have emerged from ancient ideas. At the same time, Hinduism celebrates wealth, and embraces India's new consumerist culture. Lakshmi, the goddess of wealth, is propitiated and pours wealth onto her devotees while she and other gods and goddesses are worshipped with ever more elaborate and expensive temples and rituals.

Hinduism's structural flexibility has allowed it to flourish in India and overseas. There is no single leader to make definitive statements, and there are few obligations which are resilient to change and adaptation. It is growing and developing as dynamically as India's economy, dubbed 'the Hindu rate of growth'. Yet

despite India's rapid modernization and often very modern outlook, the West has yet to revise its view of India, and
particularly of Hinduism, which it often regards wrongly as an
antique, unchanging religion.

2

Hindu Beliefs

Belief is not central to Hinduism. There is no declaration of faith or set of principles to follow and much of Hinduism is based on other forms of understanding, such as logic and analytic thought. However, there are some key beliefs about how the world is and how it should be. These include a view of the world order (*dharma*), of actions and their consequences (*karma*), the soul and its transmigration (*samsara*) and release (*moksha* or *mukti*). In traditional Hindu cosmology, unlike the Western linear system, time is seen as cyclical.

Many Hindus believe in the existence of a soul (*atman*), which migrates, being reborn in different bodies, both human and animal. They aim at the liberation (*moksha*) of the *atman* from rebirth (*samsara*), by freeing oneself from one's actions (*karma*).

The soul is also of great importance to one of the most debated topics in Hindu religious thought, namely the question of the identity of *atman* and Brahman. In the oldest Hindu compositions of the Vedas (composed over several centuries around the beginning of the first millennium BCE), Brahman is identified as the power of the ritual, then is later understood as the essence of the universe, and by the time the Upanishads were composed (800–300 BCE), the relationship between *atman* and Brahman is the central debate. The nature of Brahman itself has changed. By the time of the Upanishads, the debates over the relationship between *atman* and Brahman vary between a non-theistic approach where Brahman has an entirely impersonal nature, and a theistic form which has reframed the questions around relationship between god and Brahman. These debates, which continued over centuries in orthodox Hindu philosophy, as they are based more on reasoning and systematic thought than around gods and beliefs, led to later sectarian divisions in Hinduism as to whether the soul is identical to Brahman, partially identical or non-identical. The monistic view of identity has little or no room for a deity, whereas more theistic forms argue that Brahman and *atman* are different.

Dharma is usually roughly translated as religion nowadays, but it also covers many concepts in Hindu thought such as duty, law, ethics, truth, moral order and cosmic order. Much of Hindu law looks to the *Manusmriti* (from the second or third century CE), a prescriptive text of ideals of what the world should be like. Most people use the term *dharma* in two ways, first, on a large scale as a way of seeing natural right, the way the world should be, and second, individual *dharma*, that is, one's own place in the scheme of the world.

The Bhagavad Gita, a key text of Hinduism, reminds us how important the performance of our duty is:

One's own duty, though defective, is better than another's duty well performed. Death in [performing] one's own duty is preferable; the [performance of the] duty of others is dangerous.

Bhagavad Gita 3.35*

* *Sacred Books of the East*, Vol. 8 (1882), (http://www.sacred-texts.com/hin/sbe08/sbe0805.htm)

A common link between Hinduism, Jainism and Buddhism is a belief in *karma*, or the idea that one's actions bear fruit. The meaning of *karma* varies historically and across communities, but broadly speaking it is an impersonal force that lies beyond the will of the gods. In other words, human actions are regulated by superhuman laws. It is generally held to exist across births, so what may look unjust in one's present life is actually a result of *karma*, the consequences of actions in an earlier life.

Most Hindus believe in fate and destiny, and that one's fate is written on one's forehead at birth. What is written depends on one's *karma* from a previous birth, but fate is also a synthesis of natural justice and god's will, and it can be overwritten by the favour of the gods or by an individual's deeds, indeed his *karma*.

Non-violence, *ahimsa*, is increasingly central to Hinduism. It was much discussed by Gandhi (1869–1948), who used it in a broad political sense as part of his programme of passive resistance against colonial rule in India. It is also employed more widely to mean a non-violent way of living that includes vegetarianism. It is often wrongly assumed that vegetarianism is a central part of Hinduism, whereas it is confined mostly to Brahmins and to merchant castes. It is not surprising that Gandhi promoted vegetarianism, as he came from a vegetarian merchant caste and grew up in Gujarat where most of India's Jains – strict vegetarians – live.

Hinduism has a unique view of time and the universe. Time has no beginning and no end, being cyclical rather than linear. In addition to various calendars, Hindus see time in vast spans of *yuga*s (aeons). A *mahayuga* (great aeon) is 4.32 million human years, beginning with the creation of the world and ending with its destruction, after which another *mahayuga* begins. Each *mahayuga* is divided into four *yuga*s which show a progressive deterioration. We are currently living in the worst of times, the Kali Yuga, which is 432,000 years long. It was preceded by the Dwapar Yuga (864,000 years), in turn by the Treta Yuga (1,296,000 years) and the Krita Yuga (1,728,000 years). At the end of this Kali Yuga, the world will be destroyed and another *mahayuga* will begin. The gods too have their own distinct time scale and one of their days, called 'a day of Brahma' after the god of creation, is equivalent to billions of human years.

The ancient Hindu view of the universe, dating back at least two millennia, is that the earth is made of seven concentric islands, each surrounded by one of the seven seas made of different liquids such as water, wine or milk. Human beings live on the innermost island, Jambudvipa (Rose-apple, or Black-plum, island). In the middle of this island is Mount Meru, on which is the City of Brahma, surrounded by the cities of the other gods. The heavenly Ganges (Akash Ganga) flows from here to Bharatavarsha, the land of India, or the land of the descendants of Bharata, its legendary founding king, which is located at the centre of the world.

Bounded by the Himalayas to the north and the oceans to the south, India is also marked out as a holy space by sacred pilgrimage sites known as *tirtha*s or fords which help one cross from the material to the spiritual world. The most important are the four *dhama*s (abodes, temples) in the cardinal directions of north, south, east and west (Badrinath, Rameshwaram, Puri and Dwarka), the seven sacred cities (Ayodhya, Mathura, Haridwar, Kanchi, Varanasi, Ujjain and Dwarka) and sacred rivers, chief of which is the Ganges. Even today, very orthodox Hindus regard crossing the sea, or 'black water' (*kala pani*) as leading to impurity and so will not travel beyond India. In the nineteenth century, many travellers performed rites of atonement on returning to India from abroad, while others, notably the Maharaja of Jaipur, took Ganges water with him on his visit to London to avoid contamination. Many overseas Hindus still choose to return to India for important rituals, notably the scattering of human ashes, although the major temples founded in overseas Indian, or diasporic, communities are now regarded as pilgrimage sites themselves. The sacred geography of India has great resonance even today, when scientific belief upholds the Western Copernican (heliocentric) view of the universe.

These beliefs are central to most Hindus but are not absolute, nor are they a matter of faith. Reincarnation, *dharma* and *karma* in their various forms are widely shared beliefs, whereas knowledge of cosmic time and space would be known by scholars and priests. The belief in the sacred land of India is still held by many.

3

Gods and Myths

Most Westerners regard Hinduism primarily as a religion in which there are many gods. It is true that there are many gods, usually said to be 330 million, but this is not relevant to most Hindus. Very few Hindus are polytheistic, in that most worship only one god, an *ishtadevata* (chosen deity), a couple (such as Lakshmi-Narayana), a trinity (Shiva-Vishnu-Brahma) or a group of gods (such as the five canonical gods, Vishnu, Shiva, Ganesha, Surya and Devi). Many Hindus regard themselves as monotheistic and say that god has many names and forms but is one. Some Hindus are not theists and do not worship a specific god, or they worship a god at a certain festival but do not perform daily devotion.

For Hindus there is no absolute distinction between the human and the divine. Some regard gurus and godmen as divine; gods may possess human beings; they may enter man-made images of them and they may incarnate themselves on earth in human form.

Gods have mostly fixed iconographic representations, although features such as the number of arms or styles may vary. Gods are usually associated with particular features, so

Vishnu's four hands hold a discus, a conch shell, a lotus (sometimes a bow) and a mace, while Ganesha has an axe (or an *ankush*), a rope, a bowl of sweets and a rosary. Gods are associated with the animal vehicles on which they travel, so Shiva temples have an image of his bull, Nandi, outside the main shrine, looking at the image while Ganesha is usually shown with a rat at his feet. Images found in the Indus Valley Civilization in India, dating back over three millennia, seem to be representations of Hindu gods, although these identifications are open to debate.

Stories of the gods date back to the second millennium BCE. Although some versions of these texts are particularly esteemed, they are not usually regarded as having a greater truth than more recent interpretations of myths, and often the most recent is the most popular, while the oldest the most revered. The story of the life of the incarnation of Vishnu as Rama has several canonical versions in the different languages of India which are still retold during festivals, but the television story of the late 1980s is one of the best known today.

The gods and goddesses have many names and forms, some deities being regarded by historians of religion as composite figures, where a local god may be identified with a canonical deity, or where different cults have combined gods, such as the stories of Krishna-Gopala, the pastoral deity, and Krishna-Vasudeva, the warrior. Devotees are not interested in such accounts unless they conflict with their own beliefs. A notable case is the interpretation of the stories of Rama, focusing around his birthplace in Ayodhya, known as the Ramjanmabhoomi. This site was not a major focus of his cult until the 1940s, when Hindu nationalists claimed that images of Rama had manifested themselves there and demanded a temple be built on the site of a four-hundred-year-old mosque.

Historians argue that there is a lack of archaeological evidence for the birthplace of Rama but belief and history seem to be incompatible. In the 1980s, following the extraordinary popularity of the television serial of the *Ramayana*, Hindu nationalists reopened their demands and in 1992 demolished the mosque. Riots ensued (mostly in Western India) and over a thousand Muslims were killed.

Shiva (Mahadeva and Shankar are among other his names), one of the most popular Hindu gods, is a god of contradictions. On one hand, he is the mountain-dwelling ascetic, who lives with attendants and the *rishi*s (seers) on Mount Kailash in the Himalayas. He wears animal skins, is entwined with snakes, and his long and matted hair bears the crescent moon and contains the River Ganga (Ganges), as he breaks her fall on her journey to earth. In the form of Bhairava he dwells in cremation grounds; as Nataraja, he performs his cosmic dance of creation and destruction. On the other hand, Shiva is also the husband of Parvati, with whom he has an often-described erotic relationship. They have two sons, Ganesh and Karttikeya, who are worshipped in their own right.

Shiva is a paradoxical god, the 'erotic ascetic', to quote Wendy Doniger O'Flaherty. Much academic ink has been spilled writing about the tantric or transgressive side of his worship, where taboos are not only broken but are crucial, as well as the mantra path which promotes esoteric knowledge. Shiva also has a devotional, personal following, where, although still the Great God Mahadeva, he is a family man who has to deal with family quarrels. In one of his famous disputes, his father-in-law, Daksha, did not invite him to his sacrifice. His wife, Sati, went to the sacrifice but was so insulted that she immolated herself (from which the word is derived for the practice of 'suttee', where a woman becomes a *sati* by immolating herself on her husband's funeral pyre). Shiva cut off his father-in-law's head, which he replaced with that of a goat to bring him back to life. In another quarrel, Shiva cut off the head of his son, Ganesha, which he replaced with that of an elephant.

Sometimes Shiva is worshipped in an aniconic form as a *lingam*, a phallus, on which libations of milk are poured to cool its heat or energy. He is also worshipped with offerings of yogurt, honey and *bel* leaves. Devotees observe several fasts and his worship often involves the consumption of intoxicants such as *bhang*, a form of cannabis. Shiva's vehicle is a great bull, Nandi, who is also revered. Shiva's followers, the Shaivites, often wear three horizontal stripes of ash on their forehead and elsewhere on their bodies.

The most worshipped god in Hinduism is Vishnu, who appears in the Vedas, texts dating back to the second millennium BCE. He is now usually venerated as Narayana, along with his consort Lakshmi. They live in the heaven of Vaikuntha, and his vehicle is the eagle, Garuda. Followers of Vishnu in any of his incarnations are known as Vaishnavas, and they wear the V-shaped *tilak* or mark on their forehead.

Vishnu has ten major incarnations (avatars), nine of which have appeared and one which is still due to be manifested at the end of the current Kali Yuga. The first of these were animals (a fish, a tortoise, boar), then a lion-man (Narsinha) followed by a dwarf, but later they were kings. The ninth incarnation was the Buddha – not a belief held by Buddhists, although they do recognize the divinity of Vishnu. By far the most important incarnations for modern Hinduism are his seventh incarnation as Rama and his eighth as Krishna.

Vishnu became incarnate in his eighth avatar, Krishna, 5,000 years ago at the conjunction of the Dwapar and Kali Yugas. Krishna is first mentioned in early Buddhist tales, and by the

time of the Bhagavad Gita (about the second century BCE) he
was a major figure. These early texts are concerned with Krishna
the hero and Krishna the god. By the time of the *Bhagavata
Purana* (*c.* 800 CE), a new form of Krishna begins to emerge,
Krishna-Gopala, the naughty child, the cowherd and lover, the
period of his youth before he becomes Krishna the royal hero.
In this form Krishna is most adored, although this aspect of
Krishna is often considered by scholars to be a folk deity grafted
onto the other Krishnas.

Krishna's early life was in the land of Braj, through which
flows the River Yamuna, between modern Delhi and Agra. After
Devaki, princess of Mathura, married Vasudeva, it was pre-
dicted that her eighth child would kill his maternal uncle, the
wicked king Kamsa of Mathura. Kamsa put her and Vasudeva
in captivity, sparing their lives on condition that he was to be
given each of her children as they were born. This happened,
and Kamsa killed them one by one. The seventh child was
saved by being transplanted into Vasudeva's second wife, who
brought him up as Balarama or Balbir. When the eighth was
born, Vasudeva managed to escape with him and took him
across the River Yamuna to the pastoral settlement of Gokul.
Nanda and Yashoda, king and queen of Gokul, had just had a
baby girl, so Vasudeva swapped them, taking the girl back to
Mathura. Kamsa tried to kill the girl, who turned into a goddess
and disappeared.

Nanda and Yashoda raised Krishna in Gokul and the forest
of Brindaban in a pastoral idyll. The people were often threat-
ened by demons such as Putana and Kaliya whom Krishna
killed. The older gods were jealous of the worship of this
cowherd and the king of the gods, Indra, sent heavy rain as
punishment, but Krishna protected the people by lifting the
mountain Govardhan as an umbrella over their heads. Krishna

spent the rest of his time grazing his cattle while playing the flute, stealing butter and enchanting everyone in the village, especially the milkmaids or *gopi*s.

Krishna played pranks on the women, teasing them in public, making them hand over their butter and yogurt, and hiding their clothes when they bathed in the river. They were jealous of one another and of his flute, which is personified as Murali. The *gopi*s were happiest on the full-moon nights of autumn when Krishna invited them to dance by playing his flute, where-upon they ran to the banks of the Yamuna to dance the round dance with him. To forestall jealousy, Krishna took on many forms so each *gopi* thought she alone was dancing with him.

Krishna returned to Mathura to kill his wicked uncle Kamsa. He restored the true king, Ugrasena, and himself became King of Dwarka in Gujarat. From this point he is Krishna the hero and the *gopi*s are left to mourn him.

Krishna is worshipped in many forms and by many names. Some worship him as the child who steals butter (Navneet Lal); the young Krishna (Balakrishna) – and in this form in the great temple at Tirupati, in the south of India, he is known as Venkateshwara; others as the flute-player (Murali); others as he holds up the mountain (Giridhara), or in the second-richest shrine in Nathdwara (Rajasthan), in the north-west, he is called Shri Nathji.

The other major avatar of Vishnu worshipped today is Rama. In the earliest versions of the story, Rama's divinity seems to have been ambiguous, although his wife, Sita, was always a goddess associated with the earth, as shown by her name, which means 'furrow'. As Rama came to be regarded as an incarnation of Vishnu, she in turn was seen as an incarnation of Lakshmi. As such she embodies all good qualities, in particular those of the ideal wife.

There is no one original *Ramayana* or story of Rama, as the core story has been told for over two thousand years in poems, folktales and recently in television serials, in India and in Southeast Asia, in Hindu traditions and among Buddhists and Jains. There are several key versions which became hegemonic in particular times and places: the Sanskrit *Ramayana* of Valmiki (composed between the second century BCE and the second century CE), the Tamil *Iramavataram* of Kampan (ninth century CE) and the Hindi (Avadhi) *Ramcharitmanas* of Tulsidas (sixteenth century CE), and the staging of the *Ramlila*, which has contributed to making Rama the most popular deity in northern India.

Sita is won by Rama, eldest son of Dasaratha, king of Ayodhya. When the king abdicates he is tricked by his youngest wife into banishing Rama and handing his kingdom to her son. Rama, Sita and his brother Lakshmana go into exile in the forest for fourteen years. A female demon Surpanakha, repulsed by Rama when she tries to seduce him, attacks Sita, provoking Lakshmana to mutilate her to punish her for her erotic desire. Her brother Ravana, wishing to avenge his beloved sister and enticed by her tales of the beauty of Sita, carries Sita off to his kingdom of Lanka. Rama's devotee, Hanuman, the monkey warrior, finds Sita, sets Ravana's city ablaze, then brings Rama and his armies to rescue Sita. Rama takes Sita back only after she has undergone a trial of fire to prove that she is pure after living in the house of another man. Rumours persist in Ayodhya, and Rama banishes the pregnant Sita from his kingdom. She gives birth to twin boys, Luva and Kusha, in a hermitage. She asks the earth to open to allow her to return; Rama ascends into heaven.

There are variations in the telling; some concentrate on Rama and Sita's love and desire for each other, some recount

Sita's heroic deeds, such as her slaying of Ravana. Various accounts of Sita emerge in women's songs, but the predominant image is of the devoted wife, who is caught up in the domestic politics of the joint family, its members presented as realities rather than ideals. Many *Ramayanas* present a family story, with typical problems and stock characters, such as the jealous step-mother, who threatens the unity of the entire family, the foolish father, who is ensnared by a jealous wife, and the devoted younger brother. The morality of all the characters has long been debated, from Rama, who abandons his wife when her purity is questioned, to the many women who are presented in negative roles, notably Dasaratha's youngest wife, Kaikeyi, who schemes for her stepson Rama's exile. However, the story of Sita, the heroine, who embodies wifely, long-suffering devotion, is always a sympathetic character. The most popular telling of the *Ramayana* in recent years has been the version shown over many weeks on *Doordarshan*, Indian national state television, in 1986–7.

Goddesses appear relatively late in Hinduism apart from minor goddesses such as Usha (Dawn) and Vac (Speech). However, archaeological evidence pre-dating the oldest texts suggests that the cult of the goddess in India is very ancient. There are statues that could well be of goddesses found in the Indus Valley Civilization of the second millennium BCE. All goddesses are forms of Mahadevi (the great goddess) also known as the Devi, though they are usually regarded as different deities. These goddesses often have subsidiary forms and so take many other names.

There are three major goddesses: Saraswati, Lakshmi and Parvati, all of whom are married and worshipped alongside their husbands (Brahma, Vishnu and Shiva). Saraswati, the goddess of learning and of music, is more often worshipped alone as

Brahma is not the focus of a major cult, while Lakshmi is worshipped with Vishnu, usually as Narayana. On her own she is associated with wealth and one day of the festival of Diwali is dedicated to her worship. Parvati is not worshipped alone but only with Shiva, often in temples dedicated to the Devi.

The Devi is the single goddess, a deity in her own right, as important as Vishnu and Shiva, as shown by one of her most commonly used names, Shakti, or power. The married goddesses, by contrast, give their *shakti* to their husbands. Devi has many other names: she is Durga, who kills the buffalo demon Mahishasura at the event which is celebrated at Navratri or Durgapuja; Kali, the black goddess with the lolling tongue and necklace of skulls, who tramples on Shiva and is appeased by blood sacrifices and tantric worship, and Amba, the goddess who rides a tiger.

Local forms of the goddess are worshipped across India, sometimes as village deities or as forms of the Devi. For example, Gujarat has Bahucharji (who rides a cockerel), Meldi Maa (who rides a goat) and Randal Devi (the goddess and her simulacra); Tamil Nadu has Meenakshi, the consort of Sundareshwara, worshipped in the great temple at Madurai.

The goddess is also known as Mata (or regional variants, Maa, Amman, Ammoru) meaning 'Mother'. She is considered as mother to her devotees as she rarely has children of her own, apart from in her form as Parvati where she and Shiva have Ganesha and Karttikeya.

Ganesha, the elephant-headed god, is popular all over India, as the remover of obstacles, always invoked before starting a new task. In western India, the Ganesha festival at the end of the monsoon is one of the major annual festivals, and in Bombay huge images of him are immersed in the Arabian Sea. Karttikeya or Skanda is most popular in south India, where he is usually called Murugan, whom scholars suggest was originally a local deity whose warrior cult has merged with that of the family of Shiva.

In addition to these major deities, many other figures are related to these gods, including classes of semi-divine beings, such as the Nagas, or snakes, which are worshipped by many Hindus. There are popular beliefs in spirits and demons, and a complicated cult of ancestor worship. Gods are also worshipped in aniconic forms such as rock formations including caves, stalagmites and stalactites as well as various stones such as the *shalagram* (ammonite stone).

Cults often grow up around new gods and goddesses. One of the most famous of these is Santoshi Maa, the goddess who gives satisfaction, whose minor cult grew into a major one after the huge success of a film, *Jai Santoshi Maa* (1975), about how she helps her devotees. The cult attracted urban middle-class women who identified with the devotee oppressed by her in-laws and enjoyed participating in a relatively straightforward series of fasts without needing any priestly or other intermediaries.

There is no end to the number of gods and goddesses in Hinduism; Hindus may choose to worship new deities or attach themselves to new cults and gurus. Even those who are devoted to one particular deity would not repudiate the other deities, preferring to say that they regard them as relatives of their chosen god or goddess and so must be treated with respect, if not worshipped directly. Some deities are worshipped during festivals or approached for specific favours at times in the devotee's life. While some Hindus are truly monotheistic, most prefer to worship several gods, despite having allegiance to one particular form.

4

Worship and Practice

Hinduism is more concerned with orthopraxy, following established practices, than orthodoxy, following established beliefs. Hindus give great emphasis to ritual from markedly religious events (rites of passage, festivals, domestic worship, temple worship) to the less marked but highly significant practices (weddings, dress, food). In ritual, caste distinctions play a crucial role. Caste is a much-contested aspect of Hinduism, which has often been seen by non-Indians as a defining feature of Hindu India and misinterpreted as a system of great antiquity.

Caste (*jati*) is not mentioned in ancient Indian texts, although there are early mentions of the social stratification of society around the four major *varna*s (literally 'colours') from the Rigveda, where the different *varna*s or groups of persons are created out of the parts of the sacrificed body of the primeval man. This hierarchical division results in the Brahmins or priests being formed from the head, the Kshatriyas (Rajanyas) or warriors and kings from the arms, Vaishyas or people (traders, farmers) from the thighs and Shudras or servants of the other three from the feet.

PURUSHA SUKTA – RIGVEDA X. 90

11 When they divided Purusa how many portions did they make?
What do they call his mouth, his arms? What do they call his thighs and feet?
12 The Brahman was his mouth, of both his arms was the Rajanya made.
His thighs became the Vaisya, from his feet the Sudra was produced.*

Caste (*jati*) seems to have its origins in the medieval Indian kingdoms where it was a loose social order. From the eighteenth century it was greatly shaped by the British colonial administration and used by them to make sense of the unfamiliar Hindu religion. Its significance only increased after independence. Yet it is not as strict a hierarchy as the British believed it to be, and even today, caste organization is far from systematic as it varies enormously from region to region.

While *varna* remains important in the wider social hierarchy, it is *jati* that is more significant in everyday modern India as its detailed rules may have to be observed. Every Hindu has a caste, even if it is that of no caste (Gandhi called the Harijans 'Untouchables', now known as Dalits). This highly complicated structure is mapped onto the *varna* groups. One cannot change one's *jati* but a *jati* can move up or down the *varna*

*The Rig-Veda translated by Ralph Griffith (1896), (http://www.sacred-texts.com/hin/rigveda/rv10090.htm)

hierarchy, so a caste can move up from *shudra* to *vaishya*, although Brahmins remain at the top and Dalits cannot become caste Hindus. The first three *varna*s are known as 'twice-born' because of the ritual initiation that they observe, usually at puberty. Kshatriyas (often warriors and landlords) and Brahmins (all priests are Brahmins) sometimes compete for dominance in the hierarchy. The former uphold temporal power, while the latter ritual power, but both are needed to work together to uphold the law or *dharma*. There are also local dominant castes, usually non-Brahmin, that set the rules for other castes in their areas, such as the Patidar caste (whose members often have the surname Patel) which, though agricultural in origin, has become dominant in parts of Gujarat.

Dalits are often excluded from Hindu rituals and some groups are regarded not only as 'untouchable' but also 'unseeable'. These distinctions are hard to maintain in the modern world, for example in train travel, but they may be observed ritually or socially. Untouchability has been banned by Indian law since 1950, but those who belong to these classes (20 per cent of India's population), use the term Dalit, meaning 'oppressed', for their political and cultural organization.

In some areas there is little clear distinction between castes and the subcastes, both referred to as *jati*. Not all *jati*s are found in any one area, and a village may have anything between several to about thirty castes. Caste is simultaneously pan-Indian and local: Brahmins and other rankings tend to be found across the country, though there are some variations in both subcastes and hierarchies.

Caste is partly, though not as exclusively as Louis Dumont suggests in his major work *Homo hierarchicus*, based on ideas of purity and pollution, with the Brahmins, at the top of the hierarchy, being the purest. In Hindu thought, pollution arises mostly from one's body and what it comes into contact with during work while eating and in sexual relations, hence the observation of caste rules about occupation, commensality (who you eat with and what you eat) and endogamy (who you marry).

Caste is also based on traditional occupations that often involve purity and impurity. Brahmins are often scholars and cooks, as they have access to learning and are ritually pure so that all castes can eat food they have handled, while lower castes act as laundrymen and barbers who deal with impure bodily substances. Even in commercial sectors such as the film industry, carpenters working on the sets are likely to be carpenters by caste. However caste is not the sole factor in a person's social standing – money, education and other achievements are taken into account. A Brahmin may cook for a rich Vaishya merchant who has to make ritual obeisance to his servant at certain festivals, an instance when the ritual hierarchies turn the social world upside down.

Caste is preserved through marriage. Strict rules govern who can marry whom. Many marriages are arranged in order to match caste requirements, which are extremely complicated and vary from subcaste to subcaste. Children are born into the caste of their parents, and children of mixed-caste marriages do not belong to either caste.

Higher castes will not accept food from lower castes with the exception of certain items which are resistant to impurity. Food has enormous ritual importance, and there are rules about who may eat what cooked by whom. Traditionally, nothing with water may be taken from anyone from a lower caste.

Milk is the purest food and safest to eat when there is risk of pollution, while water is one of the most dangerous. Vegetarian food is purer than non-vegetarian, so many Brahmins and

Vaishyas are vegetarian, especially in Gujarat and south India, and this is regarded as a high-caste practice. This means they do not eat meat, fish or eggs, while many also avoid 'heating' foods such as onion and garlic. Brahmins are generally non-vegetarian in some regions (such as Bengal and Kashmir), as are most Kshatriyas, although they all generally abstain from beef, as they believe the cow is sacred and should be worshipped as a mother. Pork is avoided as unclean but there is no religious taboo on eating it.

A Hindu must keep his or her body free of impurities, notably excretions. Parts of the body that are removed, such as hair and nails, are polluting and must be cut outside the house and not on an inauspicious day such as a Saturday. A woman menstruating can be prohibited from the kitchen in some houses, and also from temples and ceremonies. When a family member dies, the decaying body is polluting to the family, who dress in white and observe periods of abstinence for periods of four or eleven days until the first anniversary of the death. Hindu widows are regarded as impure and are barred from auspicious functions such as weddings and festivals.

All the above observances are breached, sometimes deliberately, sometimes unknowingly, in the modern world. Someone who lives and works in a modern metropolis cannot avoid contact with other castes and outcastes in daily life when commuting, working in an office, eating in a restaurant and so on. Even rules of marriage are more flexible, although lip service will often be paid to the ideals of purity. Lower castes and Dalits tend to remain at the bottom of all social hierarchies and most workers in menial jobs will be from these communities.

A male Hindu's life is modelled on the ideal stages set out in the *varnashramadharma*. First, he will be initiated, a ceremony in which a sacred thread is tied to mark the initiation or second birth. This thread is worn for the rest of the man's life, and marks the stage of *brahmacharya* – celibacy and studenthood, when he studies the Vedas. It is now often done at puberty or at the time of marriage. After this, one becomes a *grihastha* or householder – married and bringing up children. Some bypass this stage for the third stage of *vanaprastha*, living in the forest, secluded from society, before finally becoming a *sannyasi*, or renouncer, giving up everything. The Kshatriya caste emphasizes the importance of the householder, while the Brahmin often focuses on renunciation. In society today, rather than becoming a *sannyasi*, a man will often retire from his job and hand over the household concerns to his son on the birth of his grandson.

Women's lives do not follow such ideal stages. Much-quoted verses from the *Manusmriti* or The Laws of Manu (V. 147–8), which are nearly two thousand years old, indicate that women's status in Hinduism is low:

> 147. By a girl, by a young woman, or even by an aged one, nothing must be done independently, even in her own house.
> 148. In childhood a female must be subject to her father, in youth to her husband, when her lord is dead to her sons; a woman must never be independent.*

A woman is polluted through menstruation and childbirth and so is forbidden access to sacred texts and learning. The vast majority of Hindu *pandits* (pundits, traditional scholars) are male, Brahmins from the priestly caste. Traditionally, women do

---

* *The Laws of Manu*, George Bühler, translator (1886) (*Sacred Books of the East*, vol. 25), (http://www.sacred-texts.com/hin/manu/manu05.htm)

not have access to Sanskrit, the language of many of the Hindu texts, which is also forbidden to those who are not from the twice-born or initiated *varnas*. Priests and other religious officials are nearly always male as are most of the important figures in Hinduism, although there are some female gurus.

A woman's only initiation occurs at marriage, after which she may move to her husband's home (at least in north India) and wear different clothing that marks her as married. Women are traditionally married before puberty, despite modern laws, and often provided with dowries by their parents which can bankrupt the bride-givers. A woman is known as *saubhagyavati* or 'having good luck' when her husband is alive. Widows are inauspicious and endure strict prohibitions on dress and eating, and are obliged to follow an austere existence. *Sati* ('suttee') or the immolation of widows has been illegal for nearly two centuries and was never a common practice, being confined to certain regions and castes.

In theory the Hindu wife ought to be devoted to her husband whom she should regard as a deity; this may be observed ritually but in practice women have a more complicated status. Women are often the carriers of Hindu traditions in the family as they mostly prepare and serve food, tell myths, practise rituals and bring up children in the Hindu way of life.

Celebrations accompany the birth of a male child, but not the birth of a female child. Girls are often referred to as 'guests in their parents' home', because they leave it on marriage, returning only for the birth of their first child. The illegal though persistent giving of dowries has come under much scrutiny, particularly with the phenomenon of 'dowry deaths', where the bride's in-laws torture and even kill her if her parents refuse to meet their demands.

Ideals of caste and gender relations have been upended by the rapid social changes which have taken place in India in the last century. While many still live in a traditional world, others live in a world which is, at least partially, modern. For those in the metropolitan cities, many features of caste and gender divisions are so remote from their lives as to be virtually unknown. Many widows live full lives, and many parents welcome the birth of a daughter. On the other hand, Hindu women often regard Western feminist views as a form of neocolonialism and celebrate their traditional gender role, especially their place in the family.

India has had a number of female politicians, including a Prime Minister and a President and women have occupied many of the highest ranks in society. Once again, this indicates the ever-present flexibility of Hindu thinking. However, while legislation protects the rights of women and Dalits, these groups are likely to suffer disproportionately from poverty and form a major proportion of the half of the Indian population who live on less than one dollar a day.

Samskaras or life rituals

The *samskaras* are the rites of passage which shape one's social identity, covering the whole of life from conception to death for the high-caste male (someone from the three *varnas*) but usually only fully observed by Brahmins. The first is the pregnancy ritual – now a sort of baby shower – which marks the occasion when a girl returns to her parents' home to give birth. Greater celebrations mark the birth of a boy, notably the distribution of *laddoo*s (sweets), while many parents observe birth rites – from naming the baby to the first feeding of solid food to the first haircut for boys and girls.

The next rite is initiation, when the boy is invested with the sacred thread. It takes place when the boy leaves the childhood world of women to study, but now is usually combined with marriage, at the moment where the groom declares his intentions to study in Varanasi but his mother's brother persuades him to marry and settle down as a householder.

Marriage (*vivaha*) is the initiation into life as a householder. Many women also have first menstruation rituals, which in earlier times when child marriage was practised was the sign to send the girl to her husband. Marriage in India is often arranged, where respective families consult caste and horoscopes, without the boy and girl meeting before the wedding. In urban India the ideal is now often the 'arranged love marriage', where families introduce suitable boys and girls to see if they like each other. In more traditional societies the wedding may still be the first meeting, although photographs will usually have been exchanged.

Weddings are often vastly and ruinously expensive for the bride-givers. One of the most important lifetime obligations for a man is giving away his daughter (the ceremony of the *kanyadaan*) to her husband. In the ceremony, fire acts as the witness, and the couple makes seven steps around it and offers it oblations. Weddings vary from community to community, but are enormously elaborate and expensive events with many ceremonies including the *sangeet* (song ceremonies), *mehndi* (ceremonies where henna is applied), and several feasts hosted by different family members.

In north India, the woman often moves to her husband's house, perhaps with his parents, although many now form a nuclear family. The joint family (several generations and several groups of brothers living together) is an ideal, and complicated kinship terms, such as special words for a brother's older brother and younger brother and their wives, which developed in the joint family, are still current.

Funeral rites are the last important stage in the Hindu life-cycle as they restore the family that is polluted by death to social life and send the soul on its way. These rites vary, but most Hindus are cremated with only a few groups opting for burial. The oldest son lights the pyre and the remains are usually immersed in a river at a holy place. The family have to observe rites (*shraddha*) until the eleventh day after the death and further ceremonies are held at later intervals, most importantly the first anniversary.

Worship: *puja* or *seva*

In Hinduism, worship means not just praising the deity but also entering a relationship with god. This worship may be daily or annual, domestic or in a public temple, conducted by a priest or by the worshipper himself. Worship may involve sacrifice, either non-violent (*puja* or *seva*) or violent, with an animal sacrifice (*bali*) offered to the goddess and usually only performed in north-eastern India, Calcutta in particular.

Daily worship consists of *puja* or 'paying respects'. Offerings are made to images of the gods, usually of flowers and sweets. The god may leave these as a favour (*prasad*), which worshippers then enjoy and distribute among others, while money is kept by the temple. Vaishnavas, or worshippers of Vishnu, do not use the term *puja* but prefer to call it *seva* or 'service' towards the deity. Another form of worship is the *arti* or worship with lamps. The devotee honours the god with lights and, by putting her hands over the flames, takes the light and warmth to her own eyes. This give-and-take element is seen also in the performance of *darshana* ('seeing'), when the devotee looks at the god's image through which, in turn, the god is understood to look back at her.

Worship is conducted with prayer, sometimes using Sanskrit

mantras and Vedic verses; and songs (*bhajans*, *kirtans*) which invoke the god's deeds and sing his praises.

Most Hindus keep three-dimensional images of deities in their homes, perhaps in a corner of a room or in a room set aside from the main house. These are usually anthropomorphic or at least theriomorphic (animal) images, but may also be naturally occurring forms of gods, such as stones, and painted images and colour prints of the deities. Temples, which differ in that the images are attended by priests and visited by devotees, have a single presiding deity with subsidiary shrines housing images of other deities. These images, at home and in the temple, are looked after in daily ritual, often beginning with a bath, then anointing, dressing and feeding the image. In a temple, this is the point at which the image offers *darshana* and *arti* is performed. Many more rituals are held during the day. The gods sleep in the afternoon before appearing again in the evening for *darshana* and *arti*.

Tantric worship of the gods also occurs, such as the worship of a virgin as a form of the goddess (the *kumaripuja*) practised in Nepal and Bengal. These rituals break taboos by sacrificing animals, the sharing of alcohol and intoxicants, as well as sexual congress. Some of these rituals are still conducted in cremation grounds, to the abhorrence of many Hindus.

These forms of worship are often too elaborate for Hindus who live in the modern world. Instead they pray to their domestic images of the gods and offer only burning incense on a daily basis. In joint families, the older people who have the leisure time follow the more elaborate rituals on behalf of their family. Many Hindus go to websites which offer online *pujas* to their favourite deities where they can bring up Flash images of lamps, incense and other items and make an online donation. Many attend temples for particular festivals or on certain days of the week, or combine pilgrimage with their holidays.

Festivals

Festivals are a time for celebration, fasting and feasting. They are also times for families to gather and mark new beginnings. Various festivals are kept during the Hindu year, some of which are clearly tied to an agrarian cycle such as the beginning of spring, the end of the monsoon or the beginning of winter. Not all festivals are celebrated in every part of India, so Basant is the north Indian spring festival while the Ganesha Chaturthi is celebrated most vigorously in Bombay where statues of Ganesha are worshipped, then immersed in the sea.

As well as various solar calendars (including one based on the Gregorian calendar), lunar calendars are followed throughout India. The months are divided into two parts. The fifteen days while the moon waxes is the bright fortnight, while the period of the waning moon is known as the dark part.

Diwali is one of the biggest festivals in India, and in parts of India marks the beginning of the new year. This 'festival of lights' may last for two or more days, and lamps are lit for the night before the new moon in Karttik (October/November). The lights celebrate the visit of Lakshmi, the goddess of wealth, but are also connected to Rama's return to Ayodhya after his exile. Among the several days of festivities, one is dedicated to the worship of Lakshmi, when the business communities seek her blessings for their new account books. On another day, sisters treat their brothers to a feast.

Holi is a north Indian spring festival to celebrate the end of winter. It falls on the first day of the dark half of Chaitra (March/April) although it usually begins the day before on the full moon. In Hindu mythology, Holika, the demoness, tried to burn her brother Prahlad, a devotee of Vishnu. Vishnu intervened to save him and now her effigy is burnt on the bonfire. The festival is also used to celebrate Krishna's pastoral idyll.

Holi is known as the festival of colours, and coloured water and powder are thrown by revellers who have taken *bhang*, a form of cannabis often consumed with a sweet drink. It is traditionally a time for rebellious behaviour and is very popular with young men.

At Rakhi, or Rakshabandhan, held on the full moon of Shravana in July/August, girls tie threads on their brothers' wrists to ask them for protection and to receive gifts.

Navratri is held on the first nine lunar days (nights) of the bright part of Ashwin (September/October), at the end of the monsoon. It is sacred to the Devi and celebrates her defeat of Mahishasura, the buffalo demon. The tenth day is Vijayadashami, the victorious tenth. In Gujarat, Navratri is marked by nine nights of the round-dance to the Devi, called the *garba* and the stick-dance, the *dandia*. In Bengal, this is the major festival, known as the Durga Puja (or simply the Puja), whereas in north India it coincides with the Ram Lila and the last day commemorates the victory of Rama over Ravana, whose effigy is burnt.

Temples also have their own festivals when the images of the deities are taken in processions through the town. The moving image of Jagannath, the presiding deity of the temple in Puri, Orissa, is so huge that it became the byword for an enormous vehicle, giving rise to the English word 'juggernaut'.

Pilgrimage

The Hindu world itself is sacred and pilgrimage or *yatra* (journey, pilgrimage) to sacred places has always played a key part in Hinduism. The pilgrim may visit sacred rivers, and sites on their banks known as *tirtha*s or fords, crossing places to the divine where he may rid himself of a sin, fulfil a vow or observe a ritual such as the scattering of funerary ashes. These may be particularly auspicious at certain times in the calendar or when planetary alignments are significant. The Kumbh Mela festival, the world's largest gathering, moves between Hardwar, Prayag (Allahabad), Ujjain and Nasik every three years, although the festival at Allahabad is the biggest gathering on earth and attracts millions of pilgrims from all over the world.

Other popular places of pilgrimage are the seven holy cities (Varanasi, Ujjain, Dwarka, Kanchipuram, Ayodhya, Mathura, Hardwar), the most holy rivers (Ganges, Kaveri, Godavari) or the four *dhams* (abodes in cardinal points: Dwarka, Badrinath, Puri, Rameshwaram). Pilgrimage has increased enormously in the last decades because travel around India has become more affordable and more comfortable. Some pilgrimages, however, remain austere, and entail great physical exertion and deprivation on the part of the pilgrim, such as the Himalayan pilgrimages during the monsoon when there is an annual death toll due to landslides.

Gurus and godmen

One of the popularly recognized features of Hinduism are its gurus or religious teachers, who attract large numbers of followers. Most Hindus will have a guru who may come from a hereditary line of teachers which the devotee's family has long followed, or a Hindu may choose his or her own guru because they find some particular resonance in their teaching. The gurus guide the devotee in daily life and are consulted regularly for advice.

There are many new 'celebrity' gurus, who are unusual in that they do not claim lineage from other gurus. Despite their new status they are often regarded as divine. Some claim their lineage from recent godmen. For example, Sathya Sai Baba (1926–) claims to be a reincarnation of Sai Baba of Shirdi who lived in the nineteenth century. His bestowing of miracles accounts for a major part of his popularity among the urban middle classes in India and the diaspora. Even though many of his followers are medical and scientific professionals, they suspend their rational judgement for his instant blessings which appeal to the time-poor, cash-rich generation.

Many Hindu gurus are genuinely spiritual and many are learned men and women, while others take an active role in social uplift and reform. However, there is a new crop of media-friendly gurus who attract particularly wealthy followers and travel the world in luxury, offering platitudinous homespun truths in the guise of wisdom and easy, if not evasive, answers to difficult questions. While their followers are vocal in their support, these new gurus are regarded with suspicion by many Hindus, whose views are often bolstered by police and other investigations into their activities.

5

Varieties of Belief

Hinduism varies across region, caste, gender, age and class. In talking with some individual Hindus, it becomes clearer what Hinduism means for some urban Indian Hindus from different backgrounds.

Leelaben Patel is a 58-year-old widow from a wealthy Patidar caste family who lives in Baroda (Vadodara) in Gujarat. Worship is central to her daily life and she devotes herself solely to Krishna.

Like many devout Vaishnava widows who are members of the Pushtimarg or Vallabhite sect, Leelaben spends most of her day worshipping the image of Krishna known as Thakurji (the Lord) which she keeps at home. This sect calls worship *seva* or 'service' rather than *puja* 'worship', emphasizing that god has taken on a human form. *Seva* is particularly demanding for the devotee as the image is regarded as a living child and must be attended to constantly.

Only one person is responsible for looking after Thakurji, and this is usually the oldest woman of the family. There is one daughter-in-law in this house and she keeps her own Thakurji in her bedroom and performs a much less elaborate *seva*.

Thakurji travels with his devotee wherever possible, otherwise he is entrusted to a close relative. During a woman's menstrual period, another member of the family must perform *seva*.

In Leelaben's lavish house, Thakurji has a large room with an attached kitchen and bathroom that is supplied with well-water, since this is purer than water from the tap. In this room all his food is cooked and baths taken, although his used utensils are washed with the family's other pots and pans. The entrance to the room has decorations around the doorframe, and from this point the space is sacred and even indoor footwear must be removed. Inside the room there are a number of wall-hangings depicting scenes of Shri Nathji's activities, a picture of the Thakurji and that of Leelaben's guru, and a photograph of her late husband. A number of steel cupboards house Thakurji's clothes and other articles required in *seva*, such as a swing for him to sit on in the rainy season.

The shrine itself is on one side of the room and is surrounded by paintings of the leaders of the sect, including the founder, Vallabha, and the present leaders, descendants of Vallabha who act as gurus. A large backcloth changes according to the season or festival. Thakurji spends his waking hours on a platform and moves into a small house with a bedroom to sleep. Near the shrine is the area where Leelaben performs his *seva*. There is a throne for him to sit, a bookstand with the liturgy for the *seva*, and a cassette player for playing *kirtan*s ('songs in his praise') in his *seva*.

Elsewhere in the house other paintings are garlanded as a mark of respect and are worshipped daily. An image hangs in the main kitchen, where Krishna can bless all the food, and there is one in the main entrance hall. There is a painting of the river goddess Yamuna in the family sitting room, but this is not worshipped.

Leelaben eats only food that she has prepared for Thakurji herself, apart from the *prasad* ('food that has been offered to a deity') from Nathdwara in Rajasthan, and has been blessed by Vallabha and the sect's leaders. She has a kitchen next to the shrine where she cooks separately from the rest of the family and although some help may be given by the family's Brahmin cook, she does all the preparation herself. The food is pure vegetarian, with no meat, fish, eggs, onion or garlic, and only a hint of chilli since Thakurji is a child and children do not eat spicy food. There are always at least two vegetables, a pulse and a sweet dish, served with milk and *paan* (betel leaves, a digestive), except on fast days when foods such as grains, pulses, salt and certain spices are prohibited. The food that has been offered to Thakurji is set aside till the family eats, and although this is Leelaben's only food, the rest of the family is given some to taste. This meal is prepared just once a day, and in the evening Leelaben eats only leftover milk and bread and perhaps some *prasad.*

In the morning, Leelaben rises very early, bathes and dresses entirely in silk as required for orthodox rituals; even the thread used for stitching her blouse is silk. She goes to the temple-room and begins to perform Thakurji's *seva.* The domestic ritual is similar to that performed at the *havelis,* ('mansions', as the temples are known, again emphasizing the human connection) – the image is woken, dressed, given food and so on. Since Thakurji is treated as a living child, the room can be heated should it turn cold. After Thakurji is bathed he is dressed in clothes appropriate to the season or festival. Leelaben talks to him as to a child, but only in Hindi or Braj, since he is from that area, rather than in her own mother tongue, Gujarati. After he has been dressed, he is shown his reflection in a mirror so he can enjoy his own beauty. His food is served on solid silver vessels, apart from his water, which is kept in a copper vessel. A screen is placed in front of him so he can eat in private. He is then given toys to play with and is later put to sleep in his house. This process usually takes until half-past eleven in the morning.

After a break for lunch, Leelaben spends an hour or two sewing Thakurji's clothes. These are of materials and colours suited to the season or festival. After this, she goes to the *haveli* to perform the ritual of *darshan*, 'seeing' and being seen by the form of Shri Nathji which is housed there. Although a figure of importance in Baroda, she is happy to join the other women in preparing vegetables in the temple. Sometimes the guru and his wife are in the *haveli* and followers may go into their living quarters and wash their feet and receive their blessings.

When the temple doors open there is a stampede of people for *darshan*, and everybody sings. Many of the Vaishnavas then visit each others' houses.

At this point, her grandchildren return from school and Leelaben spends some time with them, all the while making flower garlands for Thakurji. In the late evening she often reads religious books and magazines.

The older educated middle-class Brahmins of south India are traditionally among the most orthodox of all Hindus. Domestic life in their homes is usually very traditional but if they leave their home towns after marriage they often reject ritual and daily practices, although they observe a vegetarian diet. They are liberal or unorthodox in religious terms but remain socially conservative. This is certainly true of the older generation, one of whom tells me about her life. It remains to be seen how much the recent migration of highly educated south Indians to the US will follow this pattern. Some may become more conservative than the older generation who moved within India, as has been the pattern with other Indian migrant professionals.

Maithili Rao is a sixty-year-old south Indian Brahmin writer and critic from an educated upper-middle-class family. She lives in Bombay (Mumbai) with her husband and has one daughter and two grandchildren, resident in the US. Maithili grew up in Hyderabad, the state capital of Andhra Pradesh. She moved after she married Shyam, a Kannadiga Brahmin from the neighbouring state of Karnataka.

'More than being a south Indian in Bombay, what was very different for me was the socially conservative but religiously unorthodox family I married into. For a few years after my marriage, there were no religious celebrations at all, except the feasting around Diwali. We don't even observe *shraddha* [funeral] ceremonies for either of our parents, nor did we have any religious ceremony in Bombay when my mother-in-law died here, in my house.'

Maithili says that she enjoyed the familial aspects of religious celebrations, though is glad to be free from it on a daily basis:

'I missed the enveloping warmth of the many festivals celebrated in Hyderabad. The place where we lived had a lot of family living close by and it was predominantly Brahmin. So there was not much explaining to do, as I had to in Ahmedabad, Delhi and Bombay (all the places I had lived in) and the taken-for-granted customs and rituals like the many *haldi kum kum* evenings [all-women gatherings where turmeric and vermilion powder are applied to the forehead], were part of my unconscious comfort zone. I actually welcomed the freedom from Mum's insistence on things like someone in the house having to do a daily *puja*, even if it just meant lighting a *diya* [lamp].'

However, she still finds ritual comforting on occasion and enjoys the aesthetic aspects of religion, from stories to architecture and art:

'I have no desire whatsoever to go to any holy place – except if there are old temples and it is in the Himalayas or somewhere scenic. I have gone to Titwala and Siddhivinayak [Ganesha temples in and around Bombay] for special favours, and perform thanksgiving for good luck – most of it to do with our daughter. I would also light a *diya* on Tuesdays but not all that regularly. Normally, I light a *diya* for birthdays and Diwali and Dassera. Festivals mean decorating the house with *rangoli* [drawings on the floor] and *toran*s [banners over doorways] – the things I enjoy most. I do confess to lighting a *diya* or saying a prayer to Ganesha when something troubling happens or to seek a favour! There, I confess to bribing!'

When bringing up children, parents must decide what to teach them. Some elements of Hindu practice are part of everyday culture in India so many parents, whether believers or not, reintroduce selective rituals, though often in an informal manner. Most Hindus, even in India, are surrounded by other religions and often show an astonishingly relaxed attitude to their children's interest in other faiths. Many middle-class Hindu children are educated in convent schools, and they may choose to follow some parts of Christian practice and other parts of Hindu rituals, according to their own preferences and their friends' practices. This is nothing new in Hinduism – Gandhi was fond of the Sermon on the Mount from the New Testament, which he included among his regular religious readings. Perhaps the present generation is more anxious to maintain their traditions, such as vegetarianism, although some in earlier generations even encouraged their children to eat non-vegetarian food.

However, as Maithili says, religion is also about culture and education:

'As for me, I am an agnostic, I guess, and my husband is an atheist – but one who believes some religion is good for children to teach them discipline and values, and they can discard the faith bit as they become more rational.

'It was when my daughter was around four or five that we started bringing home a Ganapati [an image of Ganesha for his annual festival]. It was more for passing on to her our own childhood enjoyment of this particular festival, more so for my husband because he lived in a remote village where they made their own idol and had great fun setting up a *mantap* [a place for keeping the image]. I have never had a *pujari* [priest] coming to do the *puja*. It was more of an ad hoc affair, with the extended family over for lunch and neighbours and a few friends dropping by for *haldi kum kum* in the evening.

'Our daughter became a bit of a Ganapati [Ganesha] devotee around the time she was seventeen or eighteen – though the only prayer she knew fully was "Hail Mary". She used to attend the Wednesday novenas at a church with a friend. She fasted on Tuesdays (lots of milk, milkshakes and fruits. Nothing beats a Hindu fast!) and sometimes would go to a temple in the evening with her cousin who was a Ganapati devotee too.'

This tolerance of other religious faiths even extends to marriage for the more liberal. Maithili continues:

'We had no problems at all in our daughter marrying a Punjabi Sikh. She got married according to Sikh rites because they both wanted some sort of religious ceremony and the groom's family happened to organize the entire wedding. They are far more religious than us but they don't expect our daughter to go to a gurdwara and stuff like that.'

As a keen feminist, Maithili feels much more strongly about the adoption of a Punjabi ritual, popularized by Hindi films:

'I must say I am rather disappointed she chooses to keep *karwa chauth* [a fast for the well-being of one's husband] – I feel very strongly about the business of keeping a *vrat* [a fast] for a husband. But I refrain from imposing my views on her if she is happy doing it.'

Maithili is now facing the dilemma of what part Hinduism will play in the life of her grandchildren, who were both born and brought up in the US:

'I really don't know what I will teach my granddaughter. She knows about Diwali and Rakshabandhan [when girls tie auspicious threads on their brothers' wrists] and enjoys doing *arti* and *puja*. My daughter wants her to know that Diwali is important and as big as Christmas. I have read a couple of books on Hanuman and will probably read the *Ramayana*, *Mahabharata* and *Jataka* tales as she and her brother grow older. I don't think she knows the meaning of prayer, though she often sees her father pray before the Granth Sahib and they also have a picture of Guru Nanak, along with her mother's collection of Ganeshas. I am told both the kids enjoy listening to the CD of the Gayatri mantra – the one sung rather beautifully by Anuradha Paudwal. So I guess they will grow up into not so typical ABCD [American-Born, Confused Desis (Indian)] kids with their mother trying to teach them about India in general – not just Hinduism – and its history, while their father will no doubt teach them cricket!'

That a belief in god is not necessary is quite widespread, with some who are born Hindu wondering if they should define themselves as Hindu. But one cannot escape one's Hindu identity, as Chirodeep Chaudhuri remarks. Thirty-two-year-old Chirodeep is from the Kshatriya caste, a Bengali living in Bombay. He says that he, along with most of his family, doesn't think of himself as a Hindu. Yet his view of the world could easily be interpreted as being typically Hindu in his enjoyment of the rich visual culture of Hinduism, which is undeniably attractive to Hindus and non-Hindus alike. As a professional photographer, Chirodeep says his only attachment to Hindu practice is to the aesthetic values of the religion, although he later admits that Hinduism helps shape other aspects of his sense of identity. As a Bengali brought up in Bombay, he often visits Calcutta (Kolkata) for the Durga Puja to reaffirm his regional identity as a Bengali, to visit his family and also to enjoy the decorations, clothes, sweets and food. One of his major projects is a photographic study of the Durga Puja in his village. Unfamiliar with the great texts of Hinduism, Chirodeep wants to read the *Mahabaharata* as part of world literature and see Peter Brook's play which he has heard his friends discuss.

Santosh Thorat, a Maratha (a shudra subcaste) from a village in Maharashtra, studied in Marathi-medium education up to BA and diploma level before moving to Bombay, where he is an assistant to the well-known writer Jerry Pinto. His experience of Hinduism is very different from those described above.

Santosh's first memory of being a Hindu was being told to avoid low castes, although he was never sure if this was because of their ritual status or their low social status, exacerbated by alcohol abuse and disorderly behaviour. He also recalls images of several gods in his house, including the family goddess, one representing the ancestors, and Khandoba, a deity popular in Maharashtra and adjacent regions usually associated with Shiva. His parents made him bow to the images. He was initially reluctant to do so as part of a wider spirit of rebellion, but it soon became a habit. He says:

'I think the first time I felt that I had been stamped a Hindu was when I went to the Gram Panchayat school. That was when my certificate read, "Santosh Thorat, Hindu, Maratha". I couldn't even read it. Someone read it to me or read it aloud and that became part of my self-definition.'

It was Maharashtrian history, particularly the story of Shivaji, the good Hindu king, and Aurangzeb, the bad Muslim king that made him connect being a Hindu with a Hindu king and Indian history.

Santosh remembers a Muslim and some neo-Buddhists at his school but most of his classmates were Hindus from several castes, which he calls Brahmins, Vaishyas, Shudras (to which he belongs), as well as OBCs, SCs and STs (Other Backward Castes, Scheduled Castes and Scheduled Tribes, often grouped together as Dalits, though not necessarily 'Untouchables'). The school had an image of Ganesha and one of Saraswati and every day all the pupils, including the Muslims, said a prayer from the *Dnyaneshwari* (the Marathi translation of the Bhagavad Gita which is popular with the Varkari Panth, the major group of Vaishnavas in the region):

'I don't think any of us made the connection between the words we spoke and the gods of Hinduism. We made a connection between prayer and god but it was the personal god we carried in our heads. Our education strove to be rational, scientific, Western. So we never went very deep into mythology or into religion.'

In turn, many of the villagers, Hindu and Muslim, visited the nearby shrine to a Muslim saint.

Santosh says that everyone in the village was united by shared views but when he came to Bombay his religion became a marker of his identity, though no one cared about his caste. He thinks that caste is being used in villages as an issue to distract from real social issues such as lack of infrastructure and rural development:

'I feel that we have a hugely sophisticated and beautiful religion. It has great assimilative powers. It has the genius of being able to hold two contradictory ideas at the same time and not feel the strain of either. It has something to teach everyone. But we have let it fall into the morass of our nation's inability to contend with modernism.'

He also thinks religion is being used for political motives and deplores the commercial marketing of religions. He argues that people should learn more about other religions and stop blindly following the religious authority of self-appointed keepers of Hindu thought, many of whom he regards as hypocrites. He has great respect for one of his ancestors, Barku Thorat, a *sannyasi* ('ascetic') whose fame for giving sugar donations led to his being known as 'Sakkharwale Baba' ('sugar saint').

Santosh is not perturbed by inter-communal marriages, though he mentions that one of his female cousins married a Muslim, which caused some initial tension. He regards his religion as Indian (rather than Hindu) and his caste as human (rather than his actual *jati* or caste), and does not confuse Indian with Hindu. Santosh also complains about the institutionalizing of *bhakti* cults, notably the Varkari Panth, and he recalls vividly the *Harinam saptaha* ('week-long recitation of the names of god') that took place at a temple at the confluence of three streams, where the whole village came together to eat and to collect money for the temple.

Santosh finds religion has become a habit, in particular saying the name of god and praying at least twice a day. Sometimes he finds reciting prayers with a *jap mala* ('rosary'), very relaxing.

'I often think my Hinduism is a habit. It is so much a part of me that I don't know where it begins and my other belief systems end. I feel sometimes that even asking questions about being a Hindu is too large. However small you make the question, however specific you make it, the answer can go anywhere, can lead anywhere.'

An important figure in any discussion of Hinduism is Kancha Ilaiah, a campaigner in the Dalit-Bahujan movement (which includes the Indian Government's categories of Other Backward Castes, Scheduled Castes and Scheduled Tribes) for low castes and Dalits. He resists being defined as a Hindu in his famous and controversial book *Why I am not a Hindu*. Now a professor of political science at Osmania University, Hyderabad, Kancha Ilaiah was born into what is officially called an 'Other Backward Caste'. His critique of Hinduism is angry and impassioned, and he rejects Hindu identity, which he labels 'caste-ized slavery' imposed on low castes as part of their more general oppression. He states:

'I was not born a Hindu for the simple reason that my parents did not know they were Hindus. This does not mean that I was born as a Muslim, a Christian, a Buddhist, a Sikh or a Parsee. My illiterate parents . . . did not know they belonged to any religion at all . . . My parents had only one identity and that was their caste.'

Although it would be misleading to pretend that such a small group of people as the one above can give an overview of Hinduism, this snapshot of their religious practice (Leelaben) and thoughts on religion (Maithili, Chirodeep and Santosh) gives us some idea of the complex and often contradictory beliefs and practices under the umbrella term of Hinduism. Leelaben's total devotion to her image of Krishna may seem worlds apart from the more ambivalent views of the feminist writer Maithili, but the latter is also very culturally Hindu in her social life and family relationships. Chirodeep is attracted by the aesthetics of Hindu culture and has an intellectual curiosity about its historical documents. Santosh's views may not be representative of other migrants to Bombay, but much is revealed in his intelligent and sensitive response to growing up with a given, unquestioned, Hindu identity before moving to one of India's most modern cities. The flexibility of their views – which adapt to changing circumstances – is striking and very different from the intolerant Hindu nationalism which is a major force in today's India.

6

Textual and Other Traditions

Many Hindus believe that one of the world's earliest urban civilizations, the Indus Valley Civilization (IVC) which flourished in the second millennium BCE, was a Hindu culture. Its settlements extended beyond the Indus Valley (in modern Pakistan) and were concentrated in western India, from the Indus to modern Gujarat. Archaeologists have unearthed seals bearing some of the world's oldest writing, but it has yet to be deciphered and the images on them have not been conclusively identified as Hindu deities. Scholars argue over whether the IVC was part of Hindu culture or a pre-Hindu civilization from which some of its cults, such as that of an animal god, were later incorporated into Hindu culture.

HINDUISM AND INDO-EUROPEAN LANGUAGES

Textual and linguistic evidence suggests that Hinduism and Sanskrit do not originate in India. It seems they existed in West Asia and came to India only after the end of the IVC. A key point was the so-called 'Discovery of Sanskrit' in

Calcutta in 1786 by the father of modern linguistics, Sir William Jones. He suggested that there was a historical connection between a number of Indian and European languages. Since then, a genetic model has been used to assert that most Indic, Iranian and European languages derive from the one parent language, spoken at least 5,000 years ago, probably in the Pontic steppes. This hypothetical language is called Proto-Indo-European.

The Indian languages descended from Proto-Indo-European are the group called Old Indo-Aryan, including Sanskrit, and the New Indo-Aryan languages, which include Hindi, Urdu, Bengali, Gujarati and Punjabi. The Dravidian or south Indian languages do not belong to this family but share many linguistic features of the area, notably vocabulary.

Old Indo-Aryan seems to have originated outside India, descended from a hypothetical group of Indo-Iranian languages. The first written sources to refer to Indo-Iranians date from 1350 BCE in a treaty from Boghazköy in modern Turkey, then the capital of the Hittites, where the gods who are found in the Vedas as Mitra, Varuna, Indra and the Nasatyas, are invoked as witnesses. The Indo-Iranians are thought to have moved east, where they split into Iranian and Indic speakers.

The speakers of OIA, the Indo-Aryans, referred to themselves as arya, a word which is also used to mean 'noble, honourable'. (This is the same word used by the Nazis, and is related to the word Iran.) They are thought to have arrived in India via Afghanistan in the late second millennium BCE. While an 'Aryan invasion of India' has now been discredited, it is still unclear what the nature of the migration was.

Although Hinduism has no founder or founding text, several texts are regarded as central to Hindu orthodox beliefs. Many of these were composed and transmitted orally for millennia but have come to acquire the status of 'scripture', even for those who may have no first-hand acquaintance with them. The oldest group of texts, which include the Vedas and the Upanishads, are called the *shruti* ('revelations') and the religious beliefs and practices which the texts support are called Brahminical Hinduism or Brahmanism because its focus is on the *brahman* or the power of the ritual (to be distinguished from the priests or Brahmins).

SANSKRIT – SACRED LANGUAGE OF HINDUISM

Hinduism's sacred language is Sanskrit. Many of the most important books of the Hindus were composed in Sanskrit including the Upanishads and the Bhagavad Gita. The oldest texts of the Hindus are the Vedas (first millennium BCE), composed in Vedic (sometimes called Vedic Sanskrit), an early form of Sanskrit. The study of Sanskrit and sacred texts was traditionally restricted to high-caste males.

The Sanskrit language was fixed for all time by a grammar set out in 'the eight chapters' (*Ashthadhyayi*), composed by Panini, *c*. sixth century BCE. Sanskrit was a major cosmopolitan language in pre-modern India, where it was used for religious purposes, for scholarship and in the courts. Apart from Classical Tamil in south India, Sanskrit held this role until the rise of the use of vernacular languages in the early second millennium CE. It was replaced in many parts of India by Persian and then by English.

The Vedas

Hinduism's sacred texts, the Vedas ('books of knowledge'), the oldest portions of which date back to the second millennium BCE, are among the most ancient compositions in the world. The four Vedas, said to have been composed by priestly families, include hymns in praise of deities as well as speculations on the origins of the world. The largest and earliest of these texts is the Rigveda. Although not found in a written form until the second millennium CE, the oral traditions of India have kept many of the Vedic hymns preserved more or less intact.

The Vedic texts comprise the four *samhita*s ('compendia') of the Vedas, which can be dated to 1200–800 BCE. These are the Rigveda, which consists of hymns and prayers, the *Samaveda*, which contains sections of the Rigveda rearranged for chants, the *Yajurveda*, which includes the sacrificial formula and the *Atharvaveda*, a mixture of hymns and spells which delivers the wisdom of the Atharva priests.

Each *samhita* is accompanied by various *brahmanas* or prose texts which give a mystical interpretation of the ritual. These were composed around 800–500 BCE. They have *aranyakas*, texts which look at the relationship between the cosmic processes and humans; as well as the famous Upanishads, mystical speculations whose dates vary enormously; *vedangas*, treatises on phonetics, metrics, grammar and other forms of scientific knowledge; and ritual *sutras*, (600–300 BCE), texts for the performance of public and domestic sacrifices.

The most important texts are the Rigveda and the Upanishads. In the early texts, the focus of worship was a great sacrifice, held by the priests over several days on an area designated as sacred space. The gods were summoned to attend and the sacrificial fire, into which oblations were poured, took these offerings to the gods. The 1,028 hymns of the Rigveda are addressed to these gods. A quarter of the hymns are in praise of Indra, the warrior god who fights demons. The first hymn is to Agni, the god of fire, who links humans and gods by taking the offerings of the sacrifice. Subsequent hymns invoke ambivalent gods who are dangerous as well as benevolent, such as Rudra (who may be a prototype of Shiva), while the god Varuna who upholds *rita* (an early form of *dharma*) is usually found along with Mitra. Vishnu is addressed as a major god although relatively few hymns address him, while many hymns concern the intoxicating liquor Soma which is consumed in the sacrifice. The goddesses are mostly minor figures apart from Usha (Dawn) and Ila (the goddess of nourishment). There are also speculative hymns about the origin of the universe, and a famous lament by a gambler. The Rigveda is invaluable as a historical, a linguistic and also as a religious document. It shows the Aryans moving eastwards across north India, and tells us about their society and their technology. The *Yajurveda* and the *Samaveda* are sections of the Rigveda arranged for the liturgy in the sacrifice, while the *Atharvaveda* contains charms and spells alongside hymns to the gods.

The later Vedic period, from the sixth century BCE, was one of great philosophical speculation, at a time of worldwide upheaval associated with increasing urbanization and the spread of writing. The Upanishads include some of the earliest philosophical ideas in India, their central concern being knowledge, particularly of the relation of the individual soul to the universe and to a possible god. The oldest Upanishads date back to around the seventh century BCE, the core Upanishads being composed up to around 300 BCE. They are mostly in the form of dialogical arguments concerning the underlying principle of the universe, called Brahman, the sacred power in the sacrificial ritual. The individual soul (*atman*) is identified with Brahman, leading to the famous phrase, in the *Chandogya Upanishad*, '*Tat tvam asi*' ('You are it', meaning that the individual soul is the universal essence). The Upanishads also develop ideas of the transmigration of the soul as well as introducing theistic trends, that is, a universe with a personal god. They also underline the importance of asceticism in acquiring mystical power, a feature prevalent in later Hinduism, as the human body becomes the focus of activity rather than the Vedic sacrifice, so asceticism is more important than the sacrifice.

Some of the philosophical trends of the Upanishads are also found in the teachings of the six century BCE Shramanas ('strivers'), including Gautama Buddha, the founder of Buddhism, and Mahavira, the founder of Jainism. Hindus regard these religions as heterodox Hindu sects which reject the authority of the Vedas. Buddhism spread to many other countries but declined in India, while Jainism was preserved almost exclusively in India where it has, compared to Hinduism, very few followers.

In response to the rise of these other traditions, a Hindu 'counter-reformation' took place. 'Classical' Hinduism formed in the great Hindu kingdoms and empires of the Mauryas (*c.* 320–185 BCE) and the Guptas (320–500 CE). During this period, the major *smrīti* ('remembered') texts or the *shastras* ('law books'), and classical Indian philosophy were composed, alongside a flourishing of classical Sanskrit literature and a growth of other intellectual works.

Hindu philosophy focuses on 'man in the world', marking a turning away from the sacrifice of the Vedic religion towards classical Hinduism. Among the key elements of Hindu thought are the *trivarga* or three ends of man: *artha* ('prosperity'), *dharma* ('law') and *kama* ('pleasure'). Each of these arenas produced a major text, which are well known, though seldom read.

Kautilya's *Arthashastra*, c. 4 BCE to *c.* 4 CE, a treatise on eco-
nomics and polity, deals with the prosperity of the king and
country; Manu's *Dharmashastra* or the *Manusmriti*, 'The laws of
Manu', dating from the second or third century CE, discusses
dharma in 2,685 verses. It covers a wide variety of topics which
reveal what Hinduism and society were like at this time. Lastly,
there is the third-century BCE's *Kamasutra* of Vatsyayana, a
guide to the cultured life for the man about town, more famous
in the West for its chapters on sexual pleasure.

Other key texts of classical Hinduism are the great Indian
epics, the *Mahabharata* and the *Ramayana*. The core of the
Mahabharata was composed in the third or fourth century
BCE, though parts are much older, and it reached its final form
of 100,000-plus verses much later. It has many interpolated
texts, that is, sections already composed before being added,
such as the Bhagavad Gita. Its main story is the war between
two sets of cousins, the Pandavas and the Kauravas, who are
descended from the founder of India, Bharata. It is often said in
India that 'What is not in the *Mahabharata* does not exist',
and this text, called 'the Fifth *Veda*', remains one of the greatest
sources of stories in modern India.

The *Ramayana*, the story of Rama, an incarnation of Vishnu,
was composed around the second century BCE to the second
century CE. Again, it deals with a family feud among princes, as
King Dasharatha, Rama's father, is tricked into sending him
into exile in the forest. During this exile, Rama's wife, Sita, is
kidnapped by the king of Lanka and then rescued by Rama, his
brother Lakshman, and an army of monkeys led by Hanuman.

These epics are foundational to the other major repositories
of Hindu myth, which date from this era onwards. These are
known as the *Puranas*, or 'ancient texts', and draw on local religious forms, 'replacing' the Vedas. Most of these contain

religious and historical material in genealogies of kings alongside stories about the major gods still worshipped in modern Hinduism such as Vishnu, Shiva and the goddess. Along with the two epics, these are the key texts for theistic Hinduism, which focuses on devotion to a personal deity. Versions of these texts are still very much a part of everyday Hindu practices.

The six systems of Indian philosophy (*shad-darshana*) all accept the authority of the Vedas, the law of *karma*, *moksha/mukti*, soul (*atman*) along with *sadhana* (control of the passions) and *ahimsa* (non-injury). The six systems are traditionally grouped in pairs, including Sankhya-Yoga, whose doctrines are similar except the former is atheistic while the second acknowledges a god, Ishvara (often regarded as a form of Shiva), separate from the soul. The former (Sankhya) mentions the qualities of *tamas* (darkness), *rajas* (activity, passion) and *sattva* (goodness), which come to underlie other systems of thought, notably ideas of the body. Yoga here means concentration or control of the senses rather than merely a system of exercises.

Nyaya-Vaisheshika comprise the school of logic (*nyaya*), which is concerned with knowledge for salvation, while Vaisheshika uses logic for its theory of atoms.

Purva-Mimamsa holds that all the Vedas are true and focuses on the *Shruti* texts and their interpretation. Uttara-Mimamsa concentrates on the later part of the *Shruti* literature, i.e. the Upanishads, and is better known nowadays as Vedanta. Its major focus is the self (*atman*) and its relation to the universe, usually called Brahman the supreme entity. The school of *advaita* or non-dualism, founded by Shankara (788–820), a Brahmin from Kerala, argues that there are two planes of reality. At one level the world exists and evolves under Ishwara, a deity, but at the higher level Brahman is the only reality and the world is *maya* ('illusion'). The other schools of Vedanta are Vaishnava, that is, they place the worship of Vishnu or his incarnations at their centre, creating a bridge to the sentiment of *bhakti* ('loving devotion to god') from philosophy.

As usual in Hinduism, there is no book or orthodox text which defines the six schools, but they would be recognized as much a part of Brahminical or Sanskritic Hinduism as any other major text. The grouping in pairs is traditional as they are closely aligned yet also divergent. They were codified in the medieval period, and this grouping is taken as standard today.

The six systems of philosophy are particularly difficult to understand. While only scholars follow the subtleties of their arguments, here are highlighted the concepts that are widely held, such as Sankhya's concept of the qualities; Yoga's emphasis on concentration; Nyaya's logic and Vaisheshika's atomic theory. The last two schools, the Mimasas, are much more widely known as they pick up the Brahman–*atman* debate and relate it to new theistic ideas, notably between Vedanta and *bhakti*.

The Bhagavad Gita, a text of more than seven hundred couplets embedded in the *Mahabharata*, was composed after 200 BCE. It is one of the most read and loved texts of Hinduism and was popularized by Swami Vivekananda and Mahatma Gandhi.

It is found in the *Mahabharata* as the Great War of Kurukshetra is about to begin. Arjuna, the most heroic of the Pandava brothers, does not want to go to war as he knows he will have to kill his family. Krishna, acting as his charioteer, explains to him that the soul is immortal and death affects only the body, illustrating his argument with various philosophies. During this, Krishna tells Arjuna that there are three ways of approaching god: action (*karmamarga*), knowledge (*jnana-marga*) and the path of devotion (*bhaktimarga*).

The first path appeals to the Brahmins, but it is hard to follow since it requires one to act in accordance with one's duty but with detachment (*nishkam karma*). The second path is not suitable for everyone as it requires study and knowledge. *Bhakti* is the path that is open to everyone and is the best. It connotes sacrifice, discipline and duty and comes to mean a religious attitude to the divine, often in the form of various types of personal relationship.

The impact of *bhakti* on the formation of the religion we call 'Hinduism' was enormous and extended over the whole subcontinent as it spread from south India from the sixth century CE, flourishing in the north in the sixteenth century. The most important change was the shift towards theism or the worship of a single deity. This could be a god or goddess, such as Shiva, Vishnu-Narayana or the goddess, but was often one of the avatars or incarnations of Vishnu, usually Krishna or Rama. *Bhakti* emphasized emotion in worship, and public worship often centred on a temple in which an image of the god was housed. A key part of *bhakti* was the introduction of new popular forms of devotional songs such as the *bhajan* and the *kirtan*, and hagiographies of the new gurus and *bhaktas*. These were composed in the vernacular languages, alongside or instead of Sanskrit, as *bhakti* was initially a social reformist movement that rejected Brahminical authority and critiqued its views of caste, gender and other issues.

This Gujarati song 'Vaishnava jana to tene kahie' was popularized across India by Gandhi:

> The true Vaishnava is the one who feels another's sufferings as his own.
> Even if he helps the sufferer, he does not feel proud.
> He praises everything in the whole world, he does not speak ill of anything,
> In speech, action and thought he is steady; his mother is extremely blessed.
> He looks on everything dispassionately, he has abandoned desire, another's wife is like his mother.
> He does not speak any untruth, he does not lay his hand on another's wealth.
> Delusion and ignorance do not enter him, detachment is firm in his mind.
> He sings along with god's name, all holy places are in his body.
> He is without greed, and bereft of deceit, he has turned away from lust and anger.
> Narasaiyo says at the sight of him, the family is saved for seventy-one generations.

Narasinha Mehta (1500–1580)

The beginnings of this devotional worship, which marked a break from the earlier Vedic sacrifice or Brahminical ritual (*kar-*

mamarga) and Upanishadic and later philosophies (*jnana-marga*), is seen clearly in the early second millennium CE, in south Indian temple cities such as the Nataraja temple at Chidambaram and the Rajarajeshwara temple in Thanjavur (Tanjore) as temples housing gods. This new theism focused on the Puranic deities, namely Shiva, the goddess and on Vishnu and his ten incarnations, especially as Rama and Krishna but also other orthodox (*smarta*) deities. The king is often identified with the deity in the temple and Brahminical rituals are associated with these temples. The temples are not only religious but also the focus of the arts, such as dance (in particular the cult of the *devadasis* – female servants of the gods) and music.

All *bhakti* cults emphasize personal devotion to an *ishtade-vata* ('a chosen deity'), often a local deity with many human attributes. The devotees (*bhaktas*) of Vishnu and his avatars or incarnations surrender to his grace, while worship of Shiva is often more complex, emphasizing teaching, action, knowledge and ascetic practice. All forms of *bhakti* highlight the importance of the emotions as a mental way of connecting the human body to the (usually) embodied deity.

The *sants* are *bhaktas* who compose poems, songs and sayings that spread among their followers. Their devotion to their god, whether in human form or in the abstract form of his name or to the guru, is particularly strong, and so they themselves become venerated (though not usually considered divine) by their followers. Their lives and the miracles within them and their encounters with god are often the subject of hagiographies.

The first *bhaktas* emerged in south India, in what is now Tamil Nadu, in the sixth century. They composed songs in vernacular languages, expressing their emotional and personal love of god. The first long *bhakti* poem, dating from 550 CE, is to the god Murugan, a southern deity who is later identified as

Shiva's son, Skanda. This was followed in the seventh century by poems to gods such as Shiva and Krishna, previously associated only with north India, composed by the 63 Shaiva *bhakta*s (the Nayanmars) and the 12 Vaishnavite *bhakta*s (the Alvars).

LANGUAGE AND *BHAKTI*

The dynamic between elite and popular forms in *bhakti* is reflected in language. In early India, religious composition was in Sanskrit or forms of Middle Indian languages (the language of the Buddhist canon, Pali and Prakrits), and were composed by and circulated mostly among educated, high-caste men.

While Sanskrit remained important within *bhakti*, being the language of the key texts – in particular those associated with Krishnaism, such as its foundational treatise, the *Bhagavata Purana*, a Sanskrit composition from south India dated to the ninth or tenth century – the *bhakti* movement saw the growth of literature in the 'vernacular' languages, that is languages other than Sanskrit.

Tamil was the only mother tongue at this time with a literary tradition, the 'secular' *Sangam* (Ta. *Cankam*) literature: writings belonging to the learned assemblies of Brahmins, dating from the first century BCE. These were in two main forms, poems of war (*puram*) and love (*akam*), which created an emotional and erotic language that was taken up by the *bhaktas*. The other Indian languages had only oral literature until *bhakti* compositions appear in the Kannada language in the tenth century, then in Marathi and Hindi and other north Indian languages.

Although the early Tamil *bhakta*s are from diverse backgrounds – Brahmins, traders, peasants, washermen and fishermen, and even included a woman – A. K. Ramanujan (1999) reminds us that most *bhakta*s were male and upper-caste rather than low-caste and over the centuries *bhakti* was reappropriated by these elite groups. Whatever the higher social standing of these groups, *bhakti* poses panditry, maleness and pride as obstacles to approaching the divine. The gender issues raised by *bhakti* were very much part of its radical nature. Every regional movement has at least one female *bhakta*, often from the upper classes, who has rebelled against her background. Being male is not a privilege; indeed male saints have to overcome their maleness, perhaps needing a third gender which is neither male nor female, suggests Ramanujan. One of the ideal roles in *bhakti* is that of a woman in love with a god whom she recognizes as her husband. This brings her into conflict with her family. In defiance, she might throw away her clothes and her shame. The most famous example is that of Mira, a sixteenth-century Rajasthani princess, tying on the *ghunghroo*s (ankle bells) of the common dancer. However, in *bhakti* women are still in some sort of relationship with men, whether a male god or a male guru, and the roles of woman *sant*s are not options for many ordinary women.

One of the most popular *bhakti* poets is Mira or Mirabai (c. 1500–1547). There are conflicting versions of her biography but it is known that she was a Rajput queen who refused to live with her husband, saying that she was married to Krishna. She also claimed that attempts were made on her life, so she fled to Dwarka. Mira imagines herself as a *gopi* (cowherd) in her songs of erotic devotion to Krishna. At the end of her life, she vanished into an image of Krishna as her soul became part of him.

The king sent a letter, saying, put it in Mira's hand:
Give up the company of saints and come to live with me!
Mira sent a letter, saying, put it in the king's hand:
Give up the royal palace and come to live with the holy men!
The king sent a cup of poison, saying, put it in Mira's hand.
Regarding it as nectar, Mira drank it, her helper is the Lord of all.

Mira (c. 1550–1547)

In north India there are two major ways of relating to god through *bhakti* – *nirguna,* where the divine is 'without qualities', and *saguna,* where the form of god is important, and his image is the focus of worship. The latter group has two subdivisions according to which incarnation of Vishnu is worshipped: *bhakta*s of Rama and *bhakta*s of Krishna.

Although the Sanskrit *Ramayana* was a major text of Hinduism, the cult of Rama emerged only in the second millennium. However, in the Hindi-speaking area of north India, the devotional worship of Rama began in Varanasi with the guru Ramananda (1400–1470), who probably came from south India. It was from this sect that the most important text in north India emerged, the *Ramcharitmanas* ('The Lake of the Deeds of Rama') of Tulsidas (1532–1623), which has eclipsed other versions of the *Ramayana* in north India, at least until the hugely popular television serial made in the late 1980s. Krishna, who appears in the old Sanskrit texts, such as the *Mahabharata*, was already the centre of a cult in earlier times though it is with the *bhakti* movement that he becomes one of Hinduism's most popular gods.

In *nirguna bhakti*, god is formless and without qualities. *Nirguna* worship focuses on meditation on the name of god, rejecting external practices (ritual, pilgrimage, images) along with caste distinctions. It arose in the fourteenth century in north India, mostly in the Hindi-speaking area, unlike *saguna bhakti* which is pan-Indian. *Nirguna bhakti* is thought to have its origins among the Nath yogis, who worship Shiva as a yogi, rejecting Brahminical Hinduism, taking *nath*s – lords or masters – as their spiritual guides. This sect's most famous leader or *nath* was Gorakhnath (ninth century to eleventh century). The Nath yogis practise *hatha yoga*, which leads to a *sahaj* (spontaneous) realization of truth and revelation of the Satguru, the True Guru.

One of Ramananda's disciples, Kabir (1440–1518), began as a devotee of Rama but is best known for his *nirguna bhakti*. He was probably a Muslim by birth, belonging to a low-caste group of weavers who had converted en masse to Islam.

Kabir's famous verses emphasize personal devotion to god. The devotee must be righteous, humble, renounce the world, practise meditation and sing the praises of god, who may be called Ram and Hari (names of Vishnu) along with Allah and impersonal names such as *shunya* (emptiness) and *shabda* (sound, the word). He is claimed as a Sufi by Muslims, and as a devotee of Rama by Hindus. Many of his verses are also found in the Sikh scripture, the *Guru Granth Sahib*. (Sikhism is often regarded as a sect of Hinduism, a classification vigorously resisted by many Sikhs.) Along with Tulsi, Kabir is the best known of the north Indian *bhakti* poets and was much quoted by Mahatma Gandhi and Rabindranath Tagore.

Bhakti has features of a Brahminical form of Hinduism, associating with the royal court and the Sanskrit language, although it is often held that it was a popular, liberationist movement. The truth lies somewhere between the two, for, while *bhakti* did in part originate in key texts composed in Sanskrit, it flowered in the vernacular languages, although the association with Vedantic philosophy incorporated this form of devotion into Brahminical Hinduism. *Bhakti*'s opposition to orthodox views of caste, gender and ideas of god often mark it as radical but the glorification of its revolutionary nature and its power as a social movement can be overplayed.

The relationship between Hinduism and Islam was variable and complex during the period of Muslim rule centred around Delhi (thirteenth to nineteenth centuries). How 'Muslim' this period was is open to debate, as this was when the great flowering of Hindu *bhakti* occurred and many of its key texts were composed. Although the rulers of India at this time were Muslims, they did not convert the whole population as Islamic rulers had done in their westward expansion. Perhaps around a quarter of India's population converted, largely through the activities of Sufi and Muslim devotional cults. Although Sufism and *bhakti* are often wrongly seen as similar, cults of personal devotion are a point of contact between the faiths. Many Hindu and Jain holy sites have shrines of Muslim Sufi saints either outside their main complexes or near the threshold.

Sai Baba of Shirdi (1836–1918) is one of the most popular saints of modern India, and has a devoted following all over the country and among the global South Asian diaspora. His life and works show the combination of good deeds, right living and miracles that typify the lives of the medieval saints. The expansion of his cult after his death is unusual as few holy men are remembered so long and by so many.

Stories of Sai Baba's life and works appear in different versions among his various followers. He appeared in Shirdi (now in central Maharashtra) in 1872, aged about sixteen and dressed as a Muslim fakir in a *kafni*, or long robe, and headdress (although older images show it as white, it is now usually saffron, the sacred colour of Hinduism). He said he did not remember his origins and is claimed as both a Hindu and a Muslim, and his name Sai suggests that both origins are possible – Sai is from Sanskrit 'Swami', while Baba, a term used for some Sufi *pir*s, is also a Hindu and Sikh word meaning 'father', used for parents and gurus. The standard story is that he was born a Brahmin but brought up by Sufis, which is supported by his request to be with Brahmins at his death. He also had a Hindu guru he called Venkusa.

When he arrived in Shirdi, he wanted to stay in a temple but the priest was not sure of his Hinduness, so he lived in a disused mosque for the rest of his life. He worshipped in the style of an *arti* with lamps and incense (still performed today at his shrine by Brahmins) and also kept a constant fire, *dhuni*, a practice associated with the Nath yogis, as well as performing the Islamic *namaz* (prayers).

Sai Baba performed many miracles in his life and continues to do so now by using yogic *siddhis* (powers). His shrine at Shirdi, built around his grave in the manner of a *dargah* (tomb of a Muslim Pir or saint), shows clear Muslim origins.

He has popular appeal, requiring neither study nor fasts, simply devotion. The religious values he upheld – of living a simple life, dispensing wisdom and compassion to his followers – are common to Indian Hindus, Muslims and others.

Hinduism has always been shaped by other religions with

which it has had close contact, from Buddhism and Jainism, through centuries of Islam. However, the coming of Enlightenment modernity in the nineteenth century, which studied Hinduism historically, was to bring further changes to this seemingly unchanging religion.

7

Modern Hinduism

Although Hinduism has no established central authority, there have been attempts to formalize it, especially in the 'semitizing' of Hinduism, that is, giving it the formal features of the Abrahamic religions. Hinduism redefined itself sharply during the colonial encounter as part of a broader engagement with modernity which led to a rupture with its past. The interaction with Western culture from the late eighteenth century had a profound impact on all aspects of Indian culture, from social formations to science and culture. New views of history, literature and religion, which Indians encountered in their education system, and the introduction of print culture, changed ways of understanding the world. Many Indians became involved in social and religious reform. Changes were felt mostly among the emerging bourgeoisie, who were often vociferous supporters of new ideas.

The Orientalists
British teachers or servants of the East India Company, who worked in India in the late eighteenth and early nineteenth centuries and studied its culture and history, were known as the

Orientalists. Products of the Enlightenment, they believed in tolerance, rationalism, classicism and cosmopolitanism, rather than their later Victorian counterparts, who believed in progressivism and nationalism. All of them knew at least one Indian language and had a high regard for Indian culture, and they all interacted closely with Indians.

The Orientalists founded major institutions to promote the study of India and its languages, including the Asiatic Society and Fort William College in Calcutta, which was then the centre of British life in India. They were the first to publish ancient Indian texts, including an English translation of the Bhagavad Gita by Charles Wilkins in 1778. They also translated the Bible into Indian languages, although there was little missionary activity at this time. The most famous of them was Sir William Jones (1746–94) who codified Indian law, drawing on the Laws of Manu, and who first posited the idea of Indo-European languages based on his study of Sanskrit. Henry Thomas Colebrooke (1765–1837), Professor of Sanskrit at Fort William, was the first Western scholar to write on Hinduism, and he created the idea of a glorious past in ancient India on the model of classical Western civilization. One of the most significant events was the opening up of ancient India through James Prinsep's (1799–1840) deciphering of the oldest writing in India, namely the Ashokan inscriptions, which revealed the history of Indian Buddhism and allowed a dating of the history of Hinduism. Although none of these scholars became a Hindu, their work created the foundation for the study of ancient India and Hinduism.

Many young people, particularly those educated in English, were enthused by this 'discovery' of India's glorious past and began to reinterpret their own history and the history of Hinduism and its beliefs, often seeking a reformation by going back to the golden days, in particular the Aryan world of the Vedas, which was now shown to be distantly related to the ancient civilizations of Europe. Reformist Hinduism in the nineteenth century created much of Hinduism as we know it today. Reformist Hinduism combines traditions of ancient India with Christian elements, so the Vedas became 'Scripture', the worship of images was rejected as 'idolatry', and much emphasis was given to social reform, in particular to issues of caste, the treatment of widows and the age of consent in marriage.

The first of the reformers was the scholar Raja Rammohan Roy (1772–1833), a Bengali Brahmin who studied Arabic and Persian at Patna, Sanskrit in Varanasi and who also knew English and Hebrew. In 1828, Roy founded the Brahmo Sabha (The Assembly of Brahma), which later became the Brahmo Samaj (The Society of Brahma). This sect drew on Roy's declaration that all religions were one, combining elements drawn from the Upanishads, the Sufis, along with Deism and Unitarian beliefs. The Brahmos rejected idolatry, sacrifice and caste and the doctrine of *karma*, their religion emphasizing reason and ethics. They were also social campaigners; Roy's struggle against widow immolation (*sati*) contributed to its abolition in 1829.

The Samaj thrived under the leadership of Debendranath Tagore (1817–1905), son of Dwarkanath, one of India's first great capitalists, and the father of Rabindranath Tagore, India's first Nobel laureate. Tagore was keen to establish a monotheistic base for Hinduism, which he could not find in the Vedas, so he compiled a liturgy based on a selection of texts from various sources and also created a new set of practices including an initiation ceremony.

The Samaj flourished and nearly perished under the leadership of Keshab Chander Sen (1838–84), who joined in 1857 and immediately introduced more social, especially caste, reforms over which he clashed with Tagore. The Samaj split under the two leaders and eventually Sen's branch prevailed. Although he introduced Vaishnava elements to his group, Sen became more and more Christian in outlook until 1875, when he came under Ramakrishna's influence and developed a more mystical outlook. He subsequently took to worshipping Kali (the goddess). The Samaj divided again in 1878 when Sen contradicted the reformist arguments about the age of consent and gave his underage daughter in marriage. Breaking away from the general Brahmo Samaj, Sen formed his Church of the New Dispensation, whose name shows his increasing attraction to Christianity, although after his death this became more of a social organization.

The original Brahmo Samaj movement was favoured by the new middle classes, the Bengali *bhadralok*. The Samaj was highly prestigious and numbered many literary and cultural figures among its members, notably Rabindranath Tagore and the Oscar-winning film-maker Satyajit Ray.

The other hugely influential reformist Hindu group in Calcutta was, and remains, the Ramakrishna Mission. Highly traditional in many ways, it was also strongly influenced by the reformist trend. Its two founders were Shri Ramakrishna (1834–86) and Swami Vivekananda (1863–1902).

Ramakrishna was a poor Vaishnava Brahmin who became a priest of Kali in the Dakshineshwar temple north of Calcutta. Married as a child, he called his wife 'Holy Mother'. He had a great attachment to Kali as a mother, having visions mostly of her but also of Krishna and Jesus Christ. His mystical approach drew on tantrism and *advaita* Vedanta but his popularity was based on his personal charisma.

Ramakrishna's disciple, Narendranath Datta, later known as

Swami Vivekananda, was an educated middle-class Bengali who founded the Mission. His religious belief was largely based on *advaita* Vedantism (usually called neo-Vedantism in the group). Although he argued that all religions were equal, he felt that Hinduism had more to offer than most. His argument that India is spiritual while the West is material is still quoted today. Paradoxically, while he advocated social reform, such as service to the poor, he was in favour of keeping caste and worshipping images.

Swami Vivekananda was one of the first Hindus to teach outside of India. In 1893 he went to the World Parliament of Religions in Chicago where he preached the unity of all religions, and founded the Vedanta Society in New York. He soon returned to India where he founded the Ramakrishna Mission in 1897. Despite his early death, the Mission has remained important. Even though it is more of an intellectual than a mass movement, Swami Vivekananda's legacy is contested by different groups of Hindus who claim him as a reformer or as a proponent of Hindu nationalism.

Of similarly huge importance in northern India was the teaching of Dayananda Saraswati (1824–83), a Shaivite Gujarati Brahmin who founded the Arya Samaj in 1875. A highly orthodox *sadhu*, or wandering holy man, Maharshi Dayananda combined a programme of religious and social reforms derived from the West with an early form of cultural nationalism based on religion but also on language (he began to preach in Sanskrit but later used Hindi). He emphasized the Vedas as the ultimate authority, even claiming that all modern science could be found therein, turning away from later forms of theistic Hinduism. Some elements of his thought seem non-Vedic, such as his monotheism, his belief in *karma* and his ideas taken from classical philosophy, but he interprets other elements of Hinduism in the light of the Vedas. For example, he rejected caste but stressed the importance of the *varnas* as a social institution. Likewise he rejected image-worship, he opposed polygamy, child marriage and even allowed for widow remarriage; he also advocated education and founded many institutions of learning.

The Arya Samaj became very popular in the Punjab where Maharshi Dayananda preached and set up his headquarters in Lahore. The Arya Samaj was accused of agitating Hindu–Muslim sensitivities, notably by the allegedly forced use of the rite of purification (*shuddhi*) to readmit Muslims – who they regarded as 'converts' to Islam – to Hinduism.

In western India, dominant nationalist reformers also incorporated Hinduism into their programme of social and national reforms. Mahadev Govind Ranade (1842–1901), a lawyer, journalist and advocate of social reform in the caste system, interpreted *bhakti* as a key part of the history of Maharashtra and indeed of India. He argued that it was a 'national' unity, not least for its anti-Brahminical promotion of 'vernacular' languages and criticism of the caste system. Ranade incorporated Shivaji, the seventeenth-century hero of the Maharashtrians, who fought the Mughals and the British, into his scheme of reform and national unity, by associating him with the Varkari Panth even though he was Shaivite.

'Lokmanya' Bal Gangadhar Tilak (1856–1920), one of the heroes of India's struggle for freedom from the British, reinterpreted Shivaji's role in Maharashtrian history this time as legitimizing a violent struggle, by emphasizing Shivaji as an anti-Muslim as well as an anti-British figure. Tilak promoted him in a festival, the Shivaji Utsav, which he began in 1896, as well as in the Ganesha festival, the Ganapati Utsav, which he launched in 1894. Both festivals were intended to promote the traditionalism of indigenous, national culture and bypassed British rules about political gatherings as these were held in the name of culture and religion.

Mohandas Karamchand 'Mahatma' Gandhi (1869–1948) is probably the most famous of all Indians in the West, where he is highly regarded as a political and religious figure. Gandhi's father was a Vaishnava while his mother was a Pranami, a sect that combined Hindu and Muslim beliefs, giving reverence to Vaishnava and Islamic texts. Gandhi studied law in London, where he was interested in and influenced by the ideas of Tolstoy and a number of religious cults. He later practised as a lawyer in South Africa (1893–1915), where he developed his political philosophy, the foundation of which, although eclectic and non-communal, was something new: namely Hindu ethics.

Gandhi had no scholarly knowledge of Hindu texts and little interest in ritual and deities but he evolved his own form of ethical Hinduism, selectively drawing on texts such as the Bhagavad Gita and the *Ramcharitmanas*, and heavily influenced by the *sants* and *bhaktas* who sought social justice, notably caste reforms. He also had an interest in theosophy and other religious traditions, which formed part of his bricolage of ethics. He mixed Christian pacifism, salvation and redemption with Jain non-violence and Hindu traditions of renunciation, notably celibacy. Gandhi followed a moral path, on which *satya*, 'truth', was the highest principle; he practised *ahimsa* (non-violence); and *satyagraha* (seizing by truth; passive resistance). He thought that politics required the same moral force as his private life, and he sought to find a way to incorporate these views into his politics and his view of an ideal society, based on a rejection of modern civilization.

Gandhi was highly regarded for his morality and religiosity, which is why Tagore dubbed him the 'Mahatma' or 'Great

Soul'. Although he tried to avoid sectarianism, and often challenged orthodoxy in particular by his emphasis on caste reform, Gandhi was mistrusted by secularists and some Muslims who thought his vision of the new India, Ramrajya, the rule of Rama, was too Hindu. His tolerance and support of other religions during the freedom struggle led to hostility from Hindu nationalists, and in 1948 he was assassinated by an extremist belonging to one of their parties.

Followers of Hindutva, or Hindu nationalism, see the traditional tolerance within Hinduism as a weakness. Hindutva is now one of the dominant forms of Indian nationalism, comprising a new politics of militant Hinduism based on ethno-religious mobilization. Hindutva is not about the presence of Hinduism in Indian secular politics but rather a politics of communal identity, which has been promoted not just through its political organization or through existing religious elements of nationalism but has been advocated as part of Indian culture around communal identities built on constructions of self, community and nation, with the Muslim posed as Other.

The roots of Hindutva lie in the political party, the Hindu Mahasabha, founded in 1909 as a counterpoint to the Muslim League by Pandit Mohan Malaviya, the first Vice-Chancellor of Benares Hindu University and an Arya Samaji. He was succeeded by Vinayak Damodar 'Veer' Savarkar who defined Hindu Dharma as the religion of India and Hindutva, 'Hinduness' or 'Hindu nationalism', as its politics. It defines a Hindu as a patriotic Indian (including Hindus, Sikhs, Buddhists and Jains) who lives in India and is devoted to his or her fatherland. It is implicitly anti-Muslim (India's largest minority) and still believes in an undivided (i.e. pre-Partition) India. It was bitterly opposed to the Hindu politics of Gandhi, who was assassinated by a Hindutva ideologue.

A member of the Hindu Mahasabha, K. V. Hedgewar, founded the RSS (Rashtriya Swayamsevak Sangh – National Volunteers' Association) in 1925. It sees itself as a cultural organization but was banned by Nehru after one of its members killed Gandhi. In 1964 the Vishva Hindu Parishad (World Council of Hinduism) was formed.

The Indian state since independence in 1947 has been dominated by secularism while Pakistan, which was carved from India by the Partition of 1947, was founded as a homeland for India's Muslims. India's first Prime Minister, Jawaharlal Nehru, had very little personal interest in religion and viewed it as a potential source of political conflict. However, even during the early years of the Indian state, Hindu nationalism began to seek political gain.

In 1951 Shyam Prasad Mookerjee founded the Jana Sangh (People's Association), a Hindutva political party whose platform championed Hindi as the national language, favoured cow protection and was pro-Israel (the latter two being anti-Muslim positions). As a key part of the Janata Party coalition, it formed a government after the Emergency (suspension of the Constitution) in 1977, then reformed in 1980 to form the BJP (Bharatiya Janata Party – the Indian People's Party), which came to power in various states as well as nationally in the 1990s. Although the BJP lost the national election in 2004, it would be wrong to underestimate the growing power of Hindutva, whose supporters are drawn mostly from emerging elites in the most developed states and in the Indian diaspora.

The rise of Hindu nationalism was simultaneous with a media boom and communications revolution. Satellite and cable television entered India in 1991 and the mobile phone and the internet followed shortly after. In 1991 India adopted a policy of economic liberalization, ending years of state control, and a new consumerist age began. The BJP and its allies harnessed the media via televised religious soap operas, popular visuals and cheap technology such as the music cassette to get its message across. Religious soaps that may not have set out with a political agenda or been overtly chauvinistic have been used by Hindutva supporters to foment nationalism.

The Indian film industry has given rise to at least two 'Hindu' genres in the last century: the mythological film (tales of gods and goddesses, heroes and heroines) and the devotional (lives of the saints). A relaxation of the rules on broadcasting religious programmes in the late 1980s in India allowed the screening of 'religious soap operas', such as the *Mahabharata* and the *Ramayana*. These television epics brought the country to a virtual standstill and set new records for audience size and reach, showing once again the epics' enduring popularity. They replaced earlier popular versions, such as those published as comic strips, which in turn replaced narrations by older family members. Dire warnings about screening religious programmes were thought to have been realized when the imagery of these soaps was mobilized by Hindu nationalists as images of Hindu India's glory.

The introduction of satellite and cable television in India since the 1990s has allowed religious channels such as Aastha to spring up, and these have propelled new gurus to popularity in India and overseas through their use of media. Shri Shri Ravi Shankar (not to be confused with the musician) is frequently seen on India's new religious television channels and his teachings circulate on DVD and CD formats, while 'new age' teachers such as Deepak Chopra have become very popular. Many of these teachers are purveyors of homespun truths and aphorisms, which they equate with wisdom, but few of them have a profound training in Hindu religion or philosophy.

Many groups which follow gurus and other leaders use privately circulated media, such as weekly blessings recorded on DVD, VHS and CD that are available at community centres or via the internet. All these help reinforce the sense of a community and, in particular, speak to the many Hindus who live overseas.

Millions of overseas Indians have connected more closely to Hinduism through online *puja*s (worship) available for different deities. They can make online offerings at their favourite temples, and they can download recordings of prayers and even religiously inspired ringtones for their mobile phones. The internet disseminates knowledge of religious practices where priests and other traditional authorities may be absent, especially in the Hindu diaspora.

In India adherence to Hinduism remains strong. However, Western ideas of secularism, which evolved where Christianity was regarded as the only religion and where it had a particular historical relationship with the state, are not necessarily relevant to India. There is no need to stigmatize Hindu religious belief and practice as forms of cultural chauvinism; they can be incorporated into a politics of Indian secularism which centres on the traditional value of equal respect for all religions.

Hinduism in the West today

Several million Hindus belong to the Hindu diaspora. While there is a diversity of belief and practice within the diaspora, a dominant form has emerged, namely the Swaminarayan movement, which has come to represent the Hindu community in countries such as the United Kingdom and the United States of America.

The Swaminarayan movement was one of the last sects to arise from north India's sixteenth-century Vaishnava renaissance.

Founded by Sahajanand Swami (1781–1830), also known as
Swaminarayan, this sect has also been extremely influential.
Some five million Hindus, nearly all from Gujarat State, are
affiliated to it. In Britain, the Swaminarayan movement claims
the allegiance of around half a million Gujaratis, most of whom
are Hindu. Although those who are not members of the sect
may attend its most famous temple in Neasden, London, for
religious festivals and other reasons, the temple's regular con-
gregations are initiated members of the sect.

The Swaminarayan movement sits on the cusp of several
religious traditions. Although Swaminaryan worshipped
Narayana or Krishna, Swaminarayan himself came to be
regarded as an incarnation of Krishna and is now the major
deity of the sect. Swaminaryan theology and ritual are similar to
those of other Vaishnava sects, but it differs in its sharp division
of ascetics and householders, the centrality of congregational
worship, its emphasis on social reform and social action, the
strictness of its rules on sex segregation and its widespread use
of the Gujarati language. It pre-dates other reform sects but
seems to have much in common with these in its agenda of
social as well as religious reform.

Although the Swaminarayan movement became an important sect in western India during the lifetime of Swaminarayan
himself, much of its rapid expansion took place with Gujarati
migrations to East Africa (where they built their first temple in
1945) and in Britain, where the first temple opened in 1970.
Today throughout the world there are 350 Swaminarayan temples.

Hinduism has long interested Westerners. While the
Orientalists working in India were studying it, the academic
study of India was growing in the West. A new discipline called
Indology spread the study of ancient Indian languages and

cultures and Chairs were set up in universities across Europe and America. These scholars produced dictionaries and grammars of Sanskrit and other languages which are still in use today.

Western philosophers began to study Indian philosophies and Hinduism, with influential thinkers such as Hegel (1770–1831) and Nietzsche (1844–1900) incorporating them into their philosophy, while Jung (1875–1961) argued for India as the world's spiritual homeland.

There were also many who drew on a more spiritual approach to Hinduism. The first of these was the Theosophical Society, founded in New York in 1875 by Madame Blavatsky and Colonel Olcott, which moved to Madras (Chennai) in 1877, where it still remains. Rooted in Western occultism and psychic interactions, it drew its spirituality from 'Aryan scriptures' including those of Hinduism and Buddhism, and took on other beliefs such as reincarnation. Theosophists took an active role in the Indian freedom struggle, with one of its leaders, Annie Besant (1847–1933), becoming president of the Indian National Congress party. It has been a conduit for many ideas from Hinduism, influencing W. B. Yeats and Aldous Huxley among others. Annie Besant claimed Jiddu Krishnamurthi (1895–1986) was the Messiah for whom they had been waiting, but he broke away to teach a form of Vedanta which in turn appealed to many Westerners.

Aurobindo Ghosh (1872–1950), a Cambridge scholar, was a celebrated nationalist who fled to the French colony of Pondicherry in south India to escape the British. He attracted many Westerners to his ashram where they study his system of 'integral yoga' to restrain the mind and senses. Ramana Maharshi (1879–1950), who lived nearby in Tiruvannamali, attracted Westerners with his form of Advaita Vedanta, with its preferred form of mediation being total silence. The title of his first work set the central question of all his thought: 'Who am I?'

In the 1960s, the counterculture-seeking young Western hippies were quick to embrace Indian gurus and godmen. Foremost among these was a guru known by various names including Bhagwan Shree Rajneesh and Osho. He preached awareness, love and happiness which were to be achieved by tantric, especially sexual, practices and various forms of psychotherapies and meditation. His disciples were neo-*sannyasi*s, or renouncers, so wore traditional orange robes, although they did not renounce the pleasures of the world. Famous for a series of scandals during his years in Oregon during the 1980s, he returned to Pune, Maharashtra, where his Osho International Meditation Resort still flourishes.

The Beatles were famously associated with Maharishi Mahesh Yogi, a proponent of Transcendental Meditation which combined yoga and meditation. The late George Harrison was a benefactor of ISKCON (the International Society for Krishna Consciousness, better known as the Hare Krishnas). Although most of the leaders are Western converts, this orthodox form of Vaishnavism has attracted many Hindus of Indian origin both in India and overseas. A temple in Watford, north of London, is one of the major focuses for Vaishnava and other Hindu festivals. Other famous Western converts to Hinduism include Christopher Isherwood, who became an authority on Vedanta, while J. D. Salinger is associated with Ramakrishna.

Non-Hindus have of course practised yoga without becoming religious converts, or indeed engaging with the philosophy of yoga. Yoga teaches asceticism and meditation for spiritual understanding. In the West, yoga usually means a form of *hatha yoga*, which dates back to the fifteenth century. In its simplest form, yoga is a series of exercises with various *asana*s (postures), and control of the breath; the exercises help discipline the mind and body for meditation and ultimately worship.

Ayurveda, 'knowledge of life' has been taught by many gurus, beginning with Brahma. This system of medicine and knowledge about the human body dates back to the fourth century BCE and was practised by many Buddhists. It is based on a system of humours, *dosha*s, namely *vata*, space and air; *pitta*, fire and water; and *kapha*, water and earth. These must be balanced in the human body by diet and by treatments with herbs, minerals and metals, as well as types of massage. Popular cosmetics companies use the term for their products but many people also consult trained practitioners.

The West still remains largely ignorant of Hinduism, prob- ably baffled by its vastness and the amount of study required to learn its languages, and the various disciplines beyond the study of religions in general that are needed to understand it. However, as traditional learning of these subjects has declined in India there still are serious students of Hinduism, ancient India and Sanskrit in universities, including Hindus and non-Hindus in Western universities.

Hinduism is far from fading at the beginning of this millen- nium, both in India and in the diaspora. Even though many regard it as impossible to 'convert' to Hinduism, it is one of the world's largest religions. It remains resilient in the face of other major religions, whether historically in India (Buddhism and Islam) or in a global context (Christianity and Islam), and in the face of atheism and Western-style secularism. While some are attracted to more militant forms of Hindu nationalism, and wish to model their religion on the rise of global militant Islamism, many younger Hindus continue to follow their ancient traditions alongside new, invented traditions. Hinduism still has its seemingly unique quality of upholding its antiquity while simultaneously engaging with the modern world with its endless ability to frame new questions and develop fresh answers in response to a changing environment.

Further Reading

Babb, Lawrence and Susan Wadley (eds.), *Media and the transformation of religion in South Asia*, University of Pennsylvania Press, Philadelphia, 1995

Ballard, R. (ed.), *Desh Pardesh: the South Asian experience in Britain*, C. Hurst & Co., London, 1994

Basham, A. L., *The wonder that was India: a survey of the culture of the Indian sub-continent before the coming of the Muslims*, Sidgwick & Jackson, London, 1954

Dumont, Louis, *Homo hierarchicus: the caste system and its implications*, complete revised ed. tr. Mark Sainsbury, Louis Dumont and Basia Gulati, Oxford University Press, Delhi, 1998

Dwyer, Rachel, *Filming the gods: religion and Indian cinema*, Routledge, London and New York, 2006

Eck, Diana L., *Darsan: seeing the divine image in India*, second edition, Anima, Chambersburg, 1985

Flood, Gavin, *An introduction to Hinduism*, Cambridge University Press, Cambridge, 1996

Fuller, C. J., *The camphor flame: popular Hinduism and society in India*, Princeton University Press, Princeton, 1992

Ilaiah, Kancha, *Why I am not a Hindu: a Sudra critique of Hindutva, philosophy, culture, and political economy*, Samya, Calcutta, 1996

Jaffrelot, Christophe, *The Hindu nationalist movement and Indian politics, 1925 to the 1990s*, C. Hurst & Co., London, 1996

Keywords in South Asian Studies, http://www.soas.ac.uk/centres/centreinfo.cfm?navid=912

Luce, Edward, *In spite of the gods: the strange rise of modern India*, Little, Brown, London, 2006

Madan, T. N., *Modern myths, locked minds: secularism and fundamentalism in India*, Oxford University Press, Delhi, 1997

Metcalf, Barbara D. and Thomas R. Metcalf, *A concise history of India*, Cambridge University Press, Cambridge, 2002

Nandy, Ashis, 'An anti-secularist manifesto' from *The Romance of the State and the Fate of Dissent in the Tropics*, Oxford University Press, Delhi, 2003, pp. 34–60

O'Flaherty, Wendy Doniger, *Asceticism and Eroticism in the Mythology of Shiva*, Oxford University Press, London, 1973

Ramanujan, A. K., *Speaking of Shiva*, Penguin, Harmondsworth, 1973

Ramanujan, A. K., *Hymns for the Drowning: Poems for Visnu*, Princeton University Press, Princeton, 1981

Ramanujan, A. K., *Collected essays of A. K. Ramanujan*. Ed. Vinay Dharwadker, Oxford University Press, Delhi, 1999

Richman, Paula, *Many Ramayanas: the diversity of a narrative tradition in South Asia*, University of California Press, Berkeley, 1991

Index